**Better Homes
&Gardens.**

CHRISTMAS
FROM THE HEART.

Volume 30

Meredith. Consumer Marketing
Des Moines, Iowa

CHRISTMAS
FROM THE HEART.

MEREDITH OPERATIONS CORPORATION CONSUMER MARKETING
Director of Direct Marketing-Books: Daniel Fagan
Marketing Operations Manager: Max Daily
Assistant Marketing Manager: Kylie Dazzo
Content Manager: Julie Doll
Senior Production Manager: Liza Ward

WATERBURY PUBLICATIONS, INC.
Editorial Director: Lisa Kingsley
Creative Director: Ken Carlson
Associate Editor: Tricia Bergman
Associate Design Director: Doug Samuelson
Production Assistant: Mindy Samuelson
Contributing Editor: Carol Field Dahlstrom
Contributing Copy Editor: Andrea Cooley
Contributing Proofreader: Carrie Truesdell
Contributing Photographers: Jacob Fox, Jason Donnelly, Marty Baldwin, Dera Burreson, Rachel Marek

BETTER HOMES & GARDENS MAGAZINE
Editor in Chief: Stephen Orr
Executive Editor: Oma Blaise Ford
Managing Editor: Gregory H. Kayko
Creative Director: Jennifer D. Madara
Food Editor: Jan Miller

Contents

A CHRISTMAS WELCOME

Your holiday home is the focal point for all the marvelous activity that comes with celebrating this magical season. Best friends come to call, family gathers, and everyone feels the warmth of this time together.

In this volume of *Christmas from the Heart,* we've given you festive do-it-yourself projects, fresh decorating tips to showcase your talents, and tasty goodies from the kitchen to make your home a warm and inviting place.

Welcome Santa, as well as friends and family, with homemade cookies by the dozen. Stir up some yummy Chocolate Blossoms with the kids and make plenty of Gingerbread Snowflakes for a cookie exchange. Bake fragrant Lavender Shortbread Cookies to share with neighbors when they drop by. Make your holiday party a no-fuss celebration with one-pan recipes your guests are sure to love. Serve Sweet-Spicy Barbecue Chicken Melts with Roasted Tomato and Bread Toss. Having a Christmas caroling party? Come in from the cold to be greeted by piping hot Cheesy Beer and Bacon Soup or Turkey and Wild Rice Soup served with your favorite baguette. They'll be sure to ask for more!

Try your hand at making a Santa pillow that the Old Elf himself would love or a too-cute-to-melt snowman appliqué quilt. Whether you live in a modern farmhouse or just love the look, you'll want to make Shimmering Farmhouse Candles for your centerpiece, Chalkboard Advent Packages for each day of the month, and a cozy Doggy Wagon Bed for that special puppy in your life. Play Christmas tunes as you wrap those special gifts in clever fabric wraps or glittering star-stamped papers. If you love the color green, you'll be inspired with handsome green candles, marbleized paper trees, and an elegant all-in-green wreath. You'll love the chapter of nick-of-time ideas like Pom-Pom Place Settings and Bottlebrush Tree Favors.

As you prepare for this most wonderful time of the year, we hope these holiday ideas and festive recipes will inspire you to create the best holiday ever—a warm and welcoming *Christmas from the Heart.*

Merry Christmas!

Carol Field Dahlstrom

Comfort and Joy...

A Modern Farmhouse Christmas

Authentic farmhouse style lends itself to simple delights with the cozy yet upscale look all through the house.

FRESH AND FESTIVE

Make your home just a little bit cozier by using colors and textures from the popular farmhouse style. Come Christmastime, boxwood, pine, and fir happily deliver the raw goods for a vignette that hints at the outdoors and a crisp walk through the woods. Above the mantel, long pine needles fashioned over a wire frame make the central wreath, while more formal and tailored boxwood wreaths take up residence on the sconces. Sprigs of pine also tuck among glass canisters filled with Christmas wishes from each member of the family to emphasize the spirit of Christmas.

PAPER TREES

Tree-line your decorative holiday vision with trees in multiple sizes, shapes, and materials from wood, metal, and paper, like these textural forms.

TIMELESS TAGS

Find tags with longevity. Weathered wood tags with twine ties are sturdy and can be used year after year. Pen names in black or gold.

BEADED GARLANDS

Like a necklace with a little black dress, beaded garlands are elegant, light, and avoid the bulk and weight of a greenery swag.

ALL IS CALM, ALL IS BRIGHT

Bleached is anything but boring. Wood bead garlands gracefully swag under the mantel, and paper trees stand with stature on either end. Knitted ivory yarns come two ways: As a chunky ottoman and a more delicate throw.

CHALKBOARD ADVENT PACKAGES

Packages wrapped in black paper and decorated with simple chalk numbers and holiday motifs hold sweet surprises—one for every day of Advent.

WHAT YOU NEED

25 small boxes • Black kraft paper • Gray string or pearl cotton • Scissors • White chalkboard pen • Wood hanger • Black spray paint • Wood dowel • Wire • Fresh greenery

WHAT YOU DO

1. Wrap the boxes with black kraft paper. Tie gray string around the boxes as wrapping a gift, leaving a long length of string for hanging. Using a chalkboard pen, draw the numbers from 1 to 25 on the boxes and decorate as desired. Set aside.

2. Spray-paint the wood hanger and the dowel. Let dry. Wire the dowel to the bottom of the hanger to extend the hanger bottom. Wire fresh greenery on the hanger.

3. Tie the boxes to the bottom of the hanger in random fashion, arranging the boxes as desired.

SHIMMERING FARMHOUSE CANDLES

Candlelight makes its own design as it shimmers in these modern candles made from paper and stitches.

WHAT YOU NEED

Tape measure • Glass candleholders • Scissors • Black and white cardstock • Pencil • Ruler • Black and white thread • Sewing machine • Double-stick tape • Candles

WHAT YOU DO

1. Use a tape measure to measure around the candleholder. Cut the cardstock or heavy paper to fit around the holder.

2. Referring to the photos, above and right, use a pencil and ruler to mark the designs on the paper. Use thread or just the needle in the sewing machine to make the design.

3. Wrap the paper around the holder and secure with tape in the back. Place a candle inside the candleholder.

Never leave a burning candle unattended.

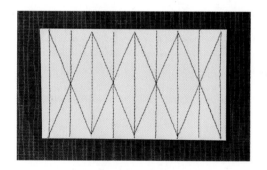

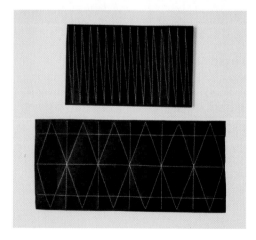

FESTIVE CHALKBOARD CENTERPIECE

A purchased chalkboard becomes the center of attention when it is embellished with Christmas motifs.

WHAT YOU NEED

Wood stain in desired color (optional) • Purchased chalkboard with wood edge • Pencil • White and red chalkboard pens • Votive candleholders and votives

WHAT YOU DO

1. Stain the outside wood edge of the chalkboard if desired. Referring to the patterns, below, use a pencil to lightly mark the design on the chalkboard. Plan your design by having the votives you want placed on the chalkboard first and plan around the votives.
2. Using chalkboard pens, draw the leaf and berry designs. Choose a few basic leaf shapes that you want to use and repeat them several times. Let dry.
3. Place votives on top of the finished piece.

Never leave a burning candle unattended.

KRAFT PAPER GREETINGS

Kraft paper gift wrap makes a perfect surface to show off exquisite hand lettering or personal-style greetings. Humble bakers twine, yarn, and string add color without fussy ribbon-tying.

WINTER WONDERLAND WRAPS

Packages wrapped in black kraft paper and tied up in strings are embellished with gentle snowflake doodles drawn on with a white chalk marker. Freehand the snowflakes knowing that no two are ever alike.

DOILY SNOWFLAKE WRAPS

The magic of making paper snowflakes unfolds into perfect patterns for simple kraft paper toppers that say "Let it Snow."

WHAT YOU NEED
Paper doilies in various sizes • Scissors • Black and natural kraft paper • Packages • Spray adhesive • Iron • Black-and-white twine or string • Small pieces of kraft paper • Fine-line black marker

WHAT YOU DO
1. To make snowflakes from doilies: Fold the doily in half, then half again, then in half again so it is in eighths. Cut triangles on folded edges. Unfold. Iron to minimize paper creases. Set aside.

2. Wrap desired packages with kraft paper. Plan where the doilies will be placed. Use spray adhesive to attach doilies to the packages. Wrap with twine. Add a note and wider ribbon atop the package if desired.

DOGGY WAGON BED

A purchased wagon is modified for your best little friend to make a soft and cuddly doggy bed for the holidays.

WHAT YOU NEED

Purchased wagon with sides • Wood dresser feet (available at hardware stores) • White paint • Water • Paintbrush • Flannel fabric • Yarn • Large needle • Pillow form • Scissors

WHAT YOU DO

1. If the wagon is new, put the wagon together leaving the wheels and one side off the wagon. If the wagon is put together, remove the front panel and the wheels. Attach the dresser feet by screwing them into the bottom of the wagon where the wheels would have been.

2. Whitewash the wood parts of the wagon by mixing white paint with equal parts of water and brushing on the wood parts of the wagon. Let dry.

3. To make the pillow, cut the fabric 6 inches longer and 6 inches wider than the length and width of the pillow form. Wrap the fabric around the pillow form, folding and overlapping the back and leaving 3 inches at each end. Thread the needle with yarn and use the running stitch to secure the back and ends. Put the pillow in the wagon.

FLANNEL GARLAND

Decorate your tree with a matching flannel garland that you can make in minutes. Cut a 36-inch x 3-inch length of fabric using a scrap of fabric from the doggy pillow. Thread a needle with red yarn and use a running stitch to sew from one short end to the other. Pull up slightly to gather and tack at the edges.

DOGGY TREAT JAR

Personalize your doggy's jar of treats with a picture of her on the container. Make a copy of her picture and cut it out. Brush decoupage medium on the back side of the picture and adhere to the front of the jar. Brush more decoupage liquid on top of the picture just to the edges and let dry. Use crafts glue to add a little trim around the picture and fill with treats.

HINTS OF HOLIDAY

An upcycled pie safe holds favorite china. During the holidays layer in just enough Christmas details to make it sing. Vintage dictionaries and a stack of plates become platforms for holiday accents. A custom print of Psalm 23 is on display all year.

SEASONAL SETTINGS

Individual place settings include black and white dishes and buffalo plaid napkins tied with a bit of greenery all placed on a wicker charger.

OPPOSITES ATTRACT

Black and white becomes the theme for this holiday gathering. A chair rail along with black-and-white plaid patterned wallpaper give the space architectural interest and dimension. The Christmas table runner showcases a hand-scripted paper scroll inked on black kraft paper.

Oh holy n
the Stars
brightly shi
it is the nigh
of our dear
Savior's birth

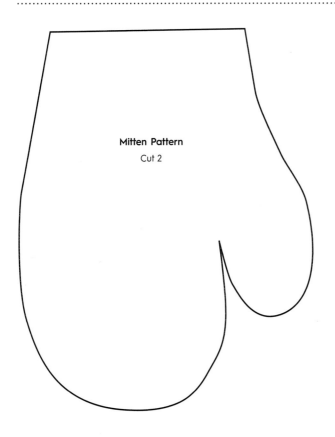

Mitten Pattern
Cut 2

FARMHOUSE MITTEN GARLAND
Miniature mittens strung on bakers twine line up to decorate a window with plenty of farmhouse charm.

WHAT YOU NEED (FOR 6 MITTENS)
½ yard each black-and-white fabric in two prints • Scissors • White thread • Black-and-white bakers twine • Small clothespins

WHAT YOU DO
1. Trace the patterns and cut out. Fold the fabric in half, right sides together. Lay the mitten pattern on the fabric and cut out. Cut 2 cuffs from contrasting fabric.
2. With right sides together and using a ⅜-inch seam, stitch the mitten together leaving the top open. Turn and press. With right sides together and using a ⅜-inch seam, stitch the short cuff ends together. Slip the cuff over the mitten, right sides together with top edges even; stitch. Turn the cuff up and tuck inside. Tack in place. Make 6 mittens. Tack mittens to a length of bakers twine. Fill mittens with desired items and use small clothespins to adjust on the twine.

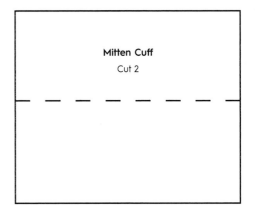

Mitten Cuff
Cut 2

MUSIC-INSPIRED TABLE SETTING

The natural hues of black-and-white music notes are the inspiration for this festive table setting. A black dinner plate and utensils are the backdrop for a black-and-white napkin tied with jingle bells and striped ribbon. A place card made from vintage sheet music finishes the look.

GIFTED PLACE SETTING

A tiny package wrapped in plaid paper is the take-home gift and also serves as the name card for this striking place setting. Steel-gray utensils and individual candles at each setting make a warm farmhouse-style welcome.

HOMESPUN TREE PILLOW

A purchased pillow becomes the star of your living room when you add a few stitches and top them off with jingle bells.

WHAT YOU NEED

Purchased pillow with open weave fabric • Pencil • Embroidery floss • Embroidery needle • Small jingle bells

WHAT YOU DO

1. Plan the design of where you want the trees stitched based on the size of your pillow. Using a pencil, mark where the trees will be stitched.
2. Thread the floss into the needle and using long straight stitches, stitch tree shapes onto the pillow. (For Stitch Diagrams, see page 158.) Sew a small jingle bell to the top of each tree.

CLOTHESPIN CANDLE

Country-style clothespins stack up to make a clever candle centerpiece for your holiday table.

WHAT YOU NEED

Glass votive with candle • Wood clothespins (See Sources, page 160) • Hot-glue gun and glue sticks • Bakers twine or ribbon

WHAT YOU DO

1. Choose a glass candleholder to fit the height of the clothespins. Plan the design and hot glue the clothespins around the outside of the glass, adjusting so they fit snuggly. Let dry. Wrap twine or ribbon around the outside of the candles.

Never leave a burning candle unattended.

COTTAGE CHRISTMAS

A potted spruce tree in a galvanized bucket sets the stage for this cozy country look.
Add texture and charm with vintage items, such as a flea market table and an old
wooden column capped with a birdhouse.

COUNTRY CHRISTMAS

A green antique window is the backdrop for a woodland display on the reclaimed mantel.
A small forest of trees (made of mercury glass, grapevines, and bottle brushes) clusters around
a barn wood star. Felt stockings are hung waiting for Santa.

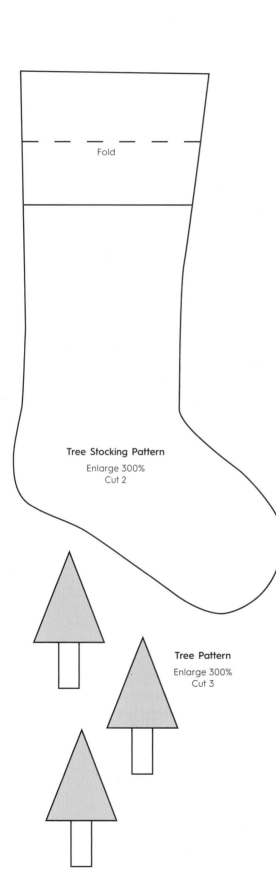

Tree Stocking Pattern

Enlarge 300%
Cut 2

Fold

Tree Pattern

Enlarge 300%
Cut 3

COUNTRY CHRISTMAS STOCKING

Creamy-white felt is sewn with wrong sides together for quick-to-make stockings for the mantel.

WHAT YOU NEED

⅓ yard cream color felt such as National Nonwovens • Scraps of felt in dark green and brown • Thread to match fabrics • Scissors

WHAT YOU DO

1. Enlarge the patterns and trace onto tracing paper. Cut out two stocking pieces, reversing one. Cut out three green trees and three brown trunks. Cut one 6×1-inch piece for the hanger. Lay the tree shapes on the stocking front where desired and topstitch in place.

2. Lay the stocking front on the stocking back with wrong sides together. Stitch around the stocking leaving ¼-inch seam on the outside of the stocking.

3. Turn the cuff down referring to placement on pattern. Sew the stocking hanger inside the stocking.

Sweet Treats...
Cookies for Santa

Say Christmas sweetly with batches of homemade cookies and bars. Santa will enjoy a plate of treats, too—simple or decorated to the hilt.

To Store Place unfilled tarts in an airtight container; cover. Place filling and topping in separate airtight containers. Store in the refrigerator up to 3 days. To serve, fill and top as directed.

HOLIDAY MOON PIE

Dreamy marshmallow cream is sandwiched between vanilla cookies then draped in chocolate to make this sandwich cookie worthy of your cookie platter. We added sprinkles for a festive look. Pictured on page 30.

WHAT YOU NEED
¼ cup shortening
¼ cup butter, softened
½ cup packed brown sugar
¼ cup granulated sugar
¼ tsp. baking soda
1 egg
½ tsp. vanilla
½ cup graham cracker crumbs
1¼ cups all-purpose flour
1 recipe Marshmallow Filling
12 oz. semisweet chocolate
2 Tbsp. shortening
   Color sprinkles

WHAT YOU DO
1. Preheat oven to 375°F. In a large bowl beat the ¼ cup shortening and the butter with a mixer on medium to high 30 seconds. Add sugars and baking soda. Beat until combined, scraping bowl as needed. Beat in egg and vanilla until combined. Beat in ½ cup graham cracker crumbs and as much of the flour as you can with the mixer. Using a wooden spoon, stir in any remaining flour.
2. Shape dough into 1-inch balls and place 2 inches apart on ungreased cookie sheets; flatten slightly.
3. Bake 8 to 10 minutes or until edges are lightly browned. Remove; cool on a wire rack.
4. Spread bottoms of half of the cookies with Marshmallow Filling. Top with bottoms of remaining cookies, bottom sides down. Arrange on a tray; cover and chill 30 minutes.
5. In a small saucepan melt chocolate and the 2 Tbsp. shortening over low heat, stirring occasionally. (Or in a small bowl, microwave chocolate and shortening, covered, 1 to 2 minutes until smooth and melted, stirring every 30 seconds.) Remove from heat.
6. Using a fork, dip cookie sandwiches in the melted chocolate mixture. Gently tap fork against rim of saucepan, allowing excess chocolate to drip off. Place on a waxed paper-lined baking sheet. Top with sprinkles or additional graham cracker crumbs. Chill at least 30 minutes or until chocolate is set. Store in an airtight container in the refrigerator up to 3 days or freeze up to 1 month. Makes 20 servings.
Marshmallow Filling For filling, in a medium bowl stir together 2 tsp. hot water and ¼ tsp. salt until salt is dissolved. Add one 7-oz. jar marshmallow creme, ½ cup shortening, and ⅓ cup powdered sugar. Beat on medium until combined.

DALGONA COFFEE TARTS

Coffee lovers, rejoice! These bite-size treats feature a buttery crust, rich mascarpone filling, and creamy dalgona coffee topping.

WHAT YOU NEED
½ cup plus 3 Tbsp. butter, softened
⅔ cup mascarpone cheese
1 cup all-purpose flour
3 Tbsp. heavy cream
2¼ cups powdered sugar
2 Tbsp. granulated sugar
2 Tbsp. instant espresso coffee powder or instant coffee crystals
2 Tbsp. warm water

WHAT YOU DO
1. Preheat oven to 350°F. In a medium bowl beat ½ cup of the butter and ⅓ cup of the mascarpone with a mixer on medium until combined. Stir in flour. If necessary, knead by hand until smooth. Shape dough into 24 balls. Press balls into bottoms and up sides of 24 ungreased 1¾-inch muffin cups.
2. Bake 12 to 15 minutes or until golden. If necessary, use the rounded side of a teaspoon to press centers of crusts down. Cool in pan 5 minutes. Remove; cool on a wire rack.
3. For filling, in a medium bowl beat the remaining 3 Tbsp. butter and ⅓ cup mascarpone with a mixer on medium until smooth. Beat in cream until combined. Beat in powdered sugar until fluffy, scraping bowl as needed. Fill cooled tarts with mascarpone mixture. Cover and chill 2 to 24 hours or until set.
4. For topping, up to 2 hours before serving, in a small bowl combine granulated sugar, coffee powder, and the warm water. Beat with a mixer on medium or whisk vigorously about 2 minutes or until light and fluffy. Spoon or pipe topping onto tarts. Chill up to 2 hours with topping. Makes 24 servings.

PEPPERMINT WHITE HOT CHOCOLATE THUMBPRINTS

Your after-dinner coffee hour is calling for these peppermint- and coffee-spiked cookies.

WHAT YOU NEED

- 4 oz. white baking chocolate, chopped
- ¾ cup heavy cream
- ¾ tsp. peppermint extract
- 1 cup butter, softened
- ¾ cup powdered sugar
- ¼ cup packed brown sugar
- 2 oz. white baking chocolate, melted
- 1 egg yolk
- 2½ cups all-purpose flour
- 1 Tbsp. instant espresso coffee powder or instant coffee crystals
- ½ tsp. baking powder
- ½ tsp. salt
- ¼ cup crushed peppermint candies

WHAT YOU DO

1. For filling, place chopped white chocolate in a medium bowl. In a small saucepan heat cream over medium just until steaming. Pour hot cream over chocolate; stir until chocolate is melted and smooth. Stir in ½ tsp. of the peppermint extract. Cover and chill in the freezer 30 to 45 minutes or until well chilled and slightly firm to the touch.

2. Meanwhile, preheat oven to 375°F. Line cookie sheets with parchment paper. In a large bowl beat butter and both sugars with a mixer on medium 1 minute. Add egg yolk, the 2 oz. melted white chocolate, and the remaining ¼ tsp. peppermint extract. Beat on low just until combined. In a medium bowl whisk together flour, coffee powder, baking powder, and salt. Gradually add to butter mixture, beating on low just until combined.

3. Shape dough into balls using 1 Tbsp. each. Place 1 inch apart on prepared cookie sheets. Press your thumb into center of each ball. Reshape as needed. Bake 8 to 10 minutes or until cookies are set and beginning to brown. If cookie centers puff up during baking, press again with the back of a small spoon. Remove; cool on a wire rack.

4. Beat chilled filling with a mixer on medium until the consistency of frosting. Spoon or pipe filling into cookies. Drizzle with additional melted white chocolate, if desired, and sprinkle with crushed peppermint candies. Makes 40 servings.

PUMPKIN SPICE SPIRALS

Make a guide for rolling out the dough by drawing the size of rectangle you need on a piece of parchment paper, then turn marked side down.

WHAT YOU NEED

½   cup butter, softened
¾   cup granulated sugar
1   tsp. pumpkin pie spice
½   tsp. salt
½   cup canned pumpkin
1   egg
1   tsp. vanilla
2¼ cups all-purpose flour
½   cup canned pumpkin
¼   cup packed brown sugar
1   egg yolk
1   tsp. pumpkin pie spice
1   recipe Cream Cheese Icing

WHAT YOU DO

1. In a large bowl beat butter with a mixer on medium to high 30 seconds. Add granulated sugar, 1 tsp. pumpkin pie spice, and the salt. Beat on medium 2 minutes, scraping sides of bowl. Beat in ½ cup pumpkin, 1 egg, and the vanilla. Beat in flour.

2. Wrap dough in plastic wrap; chill until easy to handle, 30 to 60 minutes. Meanwhile, for filling, in a small bowl combine ½ cup pumpkin, brown sugar, egg yolk, and 1 tsp. pumpkin pie spice.

3. On a floured surface roll dough to a 15×10-inch rectangle. Spread with pumpkin filling. Cut rectangle in half crosswise. Tightly roll up dough halves, starting from short sides; pinch to seal edges. Wrap rolls in plastic wrap; freeze 4 hours or until firm enough to slice.

4. Preheat oven to 375°F. Line cookie sheets with parchment paper. Cut rolls into ¼-inch slices. Place 2 inches apart on prepared cookie sheets.

5. Bake 10 to 12 minutes or until edges are light brown. Cool on cookie sheets 1 minute. Remove; cool on a wire rack. Drizzle with Cream Cheese Icing. Makes 40 servings.

Cream Cheese Icing In a medium bowl beat 2 oz. softened cream cheese and 1 Tbsp. softened butter with a mixer on medium until smooth. Beat in ¾ cup powdered sugar and enough milk (3 to 4 tsp.) to make drizzling consistency.

CHOCOLATE BLOSSOMS

Kids will enjoy rolling the balls in sugar then placing the chocolate star after baking. Omit the coffee powder if you like.

WHAT YOU NEED

4   oz. bittersweet chocolate, chopped
¾   cup shortening
¼   cup butter, softened
¾   cup granulated sugar
½   cup packed brown sugar
1   Tbsp. instant espresso coffee powder or instant coffee crystals
1   tsp. baking powder
¼   tsp. salt
⅛   tsp. baking soda
1   egg
1   tsp. vanilla
2   cups all-purpose flour
    Milk chocolate stars or milk or dark chocolates

WHAT YOU DO

1. In a small saucepan cook and stir chopped chocolate over low heat until melted. (Or microwave chocolate 1 to 1½ minutes or until melted and smooth, stirring twice). Cool.

2. Meanwhile, preheat oven to 350°F. In a large bowl beat shortening and butter with a mixer on medium 30 seconds. Add ½ cup of the granulated sugar and next five ingredients (through baking soda). Beat until combined, scraping bowl as needed. Beat in egg and vanilla until combined. Beat in melted chocolate. Beat in flour.

3. Shape dough into 1-inch balls. Roll balls in remaining ¼ cup granulated sugar to coat. Place 2 inches apart on an ungreased cookie sheet. Bake 8 to 10 minutes or until edges are firm and bottoms are light brown. Immediately press chocolate stars into cookie centers. Remove; cool on a wire rack. Makes 66 servings.

To Store Layer cookies between waxed paper in an airtight container. Store at room temperature up to 2 days or freeze up to 3 months.

MISSISSIPPI MUD COOKIES

Intense chocolate flavor, fluffy marshmallow topping, and sweet toasted pecans give this simple cookie incredible flavor.

WHAT YOU NEED

7 oz. bittersweet chocolate, chopped
5 oz. unsweetened chocolate, chopped
½ cup butter
⅓ cup all-purpose flour
¼ tsp. baking powder
¼ tsp. salt
1 cup granulated sugar
¾ cup packed brown sugar

4 eggs
½ cup butter, softened
1 7-oz. jar marshmallow creme
1 cup powdered sugar
1 cup semisweet chocolate chips
1 Tbsp. shortening
½ cup chopped pecans, toasted

WHAT YOU DO

1. For cookies, in a 2-qt. saucepan combine bittersweet and unsweetened chocolates and ½ cup butter. Heat and stir over low until melted and smooth. Remove from heat. Cool 10 minutes. In a small bowl combine flour, baking powder, and salt.

2. Meanwhile, in a large bowl combine granulated sugar, brown sugar, and eggs. Beat with a mixer on medium to high 2 to 3 minutes or until thickened and lightened in color, scraping bowl as needed. Beat in melted chocolate mixture. Add flour mixture to chocolate mixture; beat until combined. Cover surface of cookie dough with plastic wrap. Let stand 20 minutes (dough thickens as it stands).

3. Preheat oven to 350°F. Line cookie sheets with parchment paper. Drop dough by teaspoons 2 inches apart on the prepared cookie sheets. Bake about 8 minutes or until edges are firm. Cool 2 minutes on cookie sheets. Remove; cool on a wire rack.

4. For frosting, in a medium bowl beat softened butter with a mixer on medium 30 seconds. Beat in marshmallow creme until smooth. Beat in powdered sugar until light and fluffy.

5. For chocolate drizzle, in a small saucepan heat and stir chocolate chips and shortening over low until smooth.

6. Spread cooled cookies with marshmallow frosting. Drizzle with chocolate drizzle and sprinkle with pecans. Let stand until set. Makes 66 servings.

To Store Place frosted cookies in an airtight container; cover. Store at room temperature up to 3 days or freeze up to 3 months.

LAVENDER SHORTBREAD COOKIES

Lightly flavored with lavender, these buttery shortbread cookies are as pretty as they are delicious.

WHAT YOU NEED

1   cup butter, softened
⅔   cup granulated sugar
¼   tsp. salt
1   vanilla bean, halved lengthwise and seeds scraped
    (half reserved for Vanilla Glaze)*
2½ cups all-purpose flour
1   Tbsp. dried lavender buds, finely crushed
1   recipe Vanilla Glaze
    Coarse sugar or crushed lavender buds (optional)

WHAT YOU DO

1. Preheat oven to 325°F. In a large bowl beat butter with a mixer on medium to high 30 seconds. Add sugar, salt, and half of the vanilla seeds. Beat until combined, scraping sides of bowl occasionally. Beat in flour (mixture will be crumbly). Stir in the 1 Tbsp. lavender buds. Using your hands, form the flour mixture into a ball and knead until smooth.

2. On a lightly floured surface, roll dough to ⅜ inch thick. Using 2- to 3-inch cookie cutters, cut dough into desired shapes. Place 1 inch apart on an ungreased cookie sheet. Reroll scraps as needed.

3. Bake 8 minutes. Rotate cookie sheet front to back. Bake 5 to 6 minutes more or until edges are firm and lightly browned. Remove; cool on a wire rack.

4. Dip tops of cookies in Vanilla Glaze. If desired, sprinkle lightly with coarse sugar or additional crushed lavender buds. Let stand until set. Makes 36 servings.

Vanilla Glaze In a bowl stir together 2 cups powdered sugar, 2 Tbsp. corn syrup, and the remaining half vanilla bean seeds. Stir in 7 to 8 tsp. milk, 1 tsp. at a time, to make glaze consistency.

*Tip Substitute 1½ tsp. vanilla extract for each vanilla bean half.

GINGERBREAD SNOWFLAKES

Warm spices and molasses make this cookie a holiday favorite. A star cookie cutter also works well.

WHAT YOU NEED

½ cup shortening
¼ cup butter, softened
½ cup granulated sugar
1 tsp. baking powder
1 tsp. ground ginger
½ tsp. baking soda
½ tsp. ground cinnamon
½ tsp. ground cloves
¼ tsp. salt
1 egg
½ cup molasses
1 Tbsp. cider vinegar
3 cups all-purpose flour
1 recipe Powdered Sugar Icing (optional)

WHAT YOU DO

1. In a large bowl beat shortening and butter with a mixer on medium 30 seconds. Add next seven ingredients (through salt); beat until combined, scraping bowl as needed. Beat in egg, molasses, and vinegar. Beat in flour. Divide dough in half. Cover and chill 1 hour or until dough is easy to handle.

2. Preheat oven to 375°F. On a lightly floured surface, roll one portion of dough at a time to ¼ inch thick. Using a 3- to 4-inch snowflake cookie cutter, cut out dough, rerolling scraps as needed. Place cutouts 1 inch apart on ungreased cookie sheets.

3. Bake 6 to 8 minutes or until edges are firm. Cool on cookie sheets 1 minute. Remove; cool on wire racks. If desired, decorate cookies with Powdered Sugar Icing. Makes 24 servings.

Powdered Sugar Icing In a medium bowl stir together 4 cups powdered sugar, 3 Tbsp. milk, and 1 tsp. vanilla. If needed,

stir in additional milk, 1 tsp. at a time, to reach drizzling consistency.

Snow Flurries A light dusting of powdered sugar over cookies and bars is both lovely and easy to do. Simply spoon the powdered sugar into a sieve held over a bowl. Tap the sieve gently as you move it over the cookies, letting the sugar shower down. Avoid stacking, handling, or moving the cookies excessively after sprinkling.

CHRISTMAS CUTOUTS

Gel food coloring provides the widest selection of colors and doesn't affect the consistency. Try a variety of tree-shape cookie cutters to create a decorative cookie platter.

WHAT YOU NEED

1½ cups butter, softened
1 cup granulated sugar
¼ tsp. baking powder
1 egg
1 tsp. vanilla
1 tsp. almond extract (optional)
¾ tsp. salt
3½ cups all-purpose flour
   Food coloring (optional)
   Gold or silver luster dust (optional)

WHAT YOU DO

1. Preheat oven to 375°F. In a large bowl beat butter with a mixer on medium to high 30 seconds. Add sugar and baking powder. Beat until combined, scraping bowl as needed. Beat in egg, vanilla, and, if using, almond extract. Beat in salt and as much of the flour as you can with the mixer. Stir in any remaining flour. Divide dough into two or three portions; tint each portion with food coloring as desired.

2. On a lightly floured surface, roll one portion of dough at a time to ⅛ to ¼ inch thick. Using 2- to 3-inch cookie cutters, cut dough into desired shapes. If necessary, dip cutters in flour to prevent sticking. Place cutouts 1 inch apart on an ungreased cookie sheet. Reroll scraps as needed.

3. Bake 6 to 8 minutes or until edges are firm but not brown. (Adjust timing for smaller and larger cookies.) Remove; cool on a wire rack. If desired, brush cookies with luster dust. Makes 48 servings.

Striped Prepare dough as directed in Step 1. Divide dough into four equal portions. Using food coloring, tint portions various shades of green; if desired, leave one portion of dough plain. Working in batches, roll out dough portions as directed in Step 2; cut into strips of varying widths. If desired, brush strips with lightly beaten egg white and sprinkle with colored sugar(s), pressing lightly to adhere. Arrange strips next to each other and push together; lightly roll over with a rolling pin to seal. Cut out dough and bake as directed.

FUDGY STRIPED PEANUT BUTTER SHORTBREAD

These are reminiscent of the fudge-stripe cookies from childhood. Feel free to sprinkle the chocolate-coated bottoms with sprinkles or chopped peanuts.

WHAT YOU NEED
1   cup butter, softened
⅔   cup peanut butter
⅓   cup packed brown sugar
⅓   cup granulated sugar
¼   cup cornstarch
1   tsp. vanilla
½   tsp. salt
2½   cups all-purpose flour
1½   cups semisweet chocolate chips
2   tsp. shortening

WHAT YOU DO
1. In a large bowl beat butter and peanut butter with a mixer on medium to high 30 seconds. Beat in brown sugar, granulated sugar, cornstarch, vanilla, and salt, scraping bowl as needed. Beat in as much of the flour as you can with the mixer. Stir in any remaining flour. Divide dough into four portions. Cover and chill 30 minutes or until dough is easy to handle.
2. Preheat oven to 350°F. On a lightly floured surface, roll one portion of dough at a time to ¼ inch thick. Using a 2½-inch doughnut cutter, cut out dough. Place 1 inch apart on an ungreased cookie sheet. Reroll scraps as needed.
3. Bake 18 to 20 minutes or until bottoms begin to brown. Cool on cookie sheet 5 minutes. Remove; cool completely on a wire rack. In a small saucepan melt together chocolate and shortening over medium-low heat, stirring until smooth.
4. Dip bottoms of cooled cookies halfway in melted chocolate. Place on sheets of parchment paper. Drizzle tops with chocolate. Let stand until set. Makes 48 servings.

GINGERSNAP-BLONDIE BROOKIES

These cookie bars feature a light blondie layer on the bottom and a molasses-colored cookie layer on top. Every bite has the perfect amount of crispiness and chewiness.

WHAT YOU NEED

1⅓ cups packed brown sugar
½ cup butter
1⅓ cups all-purpose flour
½ tsp. baking powder
⅛ tsp. baking soda
1 egg
1 tsp. vanilla
1½ cups all-purpose flour
1 tsp. ground ginger
½ tsp. baking soda
½ tsp. ground cinnamon
¼ tsp. ground cloves
   Pinch of salt
½ cup butter, softened
⅔ cup granulated sugar
1 egg
3 Tbsp. molasses
1 Tbsp. coarse sugar

WHAT YOU DO

1. For blondies, in a medium saucepan cook and stir brown sugar and ½ cup butter over medium until melted and smooth, stirring frequently. Cool 10 minutes.

2. Preheat oven to 350°F. Line a 9-inch square baking pan with foil, extending foil over edges. Grease foil. In a medium bowl stir together 1⅓ cups flour, the baking powder, and ⅛ tsp. baking soda. Stir 1 egg and the vanilla into brown sugar mixture. Stir in flour mixture. Spread batter in prepared pan.

3. For cookies, in a medium bowl stir together next six ingredients (through salt). In a large bowl beat softened butter with a mixer on low 30 seconds. Add granulated sugar; beat until combined. Beat in remaining egg and the molasses until combined. Beat in as much of the flour mixture as you can with the mixer. Stir in any remaining flour mixture.

4. Crumble cookie dough over blondie batter in pan. Sprinkle coarse sugar over top. Bake 30 minutes or until browned and set. Cool in pan on a wire rack. Using foil, lift out uncut bars. Cut into bars. Makes 32 servings.

PEANUT BUTTER AND "OREO" BROOKIES

Part cookies- and cream-brownies, part peanut butter cookies, this tender treat will be a welcome addition to a cookie exchange.

WHAT YOU NEED
- ¾ cup butter, softened
- ¾ cup packed brown sugar
- ½ tsp. baking soda
- ½ tsp. salt
- 1 egg
- 1½ tsp. vanilla
- ¼ cup unsweetened cocoa powder
- 1 cup all-purpose flour
- 1½ cups chopped chocolate sandwich cookies with white filling (about 15 cookies)
- ½ cup creamy peanut butter
- ¾ cup butter, softened
- ¾ cup packed brown sugar
- ½ tsp. baking soda
- ½ tsp. baking powder
- 1 egg
- ½ tsp. vanilla
- 1 cup all-purpose flour
- ½ cup chopped peanuts

WHAT YOU DO

1. Preheat oven to 375°F. For brownies, in a large bowl beat ¾ cup butter on medium to high 30 seconds. Add ¾ cup brown sugar, ½ tsp. baking soda, and salt. Beat on medium 2 minutes, scraping bowl as needed. Beat in 1 egg and 1½ tsp. vanilla until combined. Add cocoa powder and beat in as much of 1 cup flour as you can with the mixer. Stir in remaining flour. Carefully stir in chopped cookies. Set dough aside.

2. For cookies, in a large bowl beat peanut butter and ¾ cup butter with a mixer on medium to high 30 seconds. Add ¾ cup brown sugar, ½ tsp. baking soda, and baking powder. Beat until combined, scraping bowl as needed. Beat in remaining egg and vanilla until combined. Beat in as much of the 1 cup flour as you can with the mixer. Stir in any remaining flour and the chopped peanuts.

3. For each brookie, press tablespoon-size pieces of each dough together and roll into a ball. Place 2 inches apart on ungreased cookie sheets. Bake 7 to 9 minutes or until edges are light brown and firm. Gently tap cookie sheets on the counter to flatten cookies. Let cool on cookie sheets 5 minutes. Remove; cool on a wire rack. Makes 36 servings.

CAKE BATTER PUPPY CHOW BARS

Make your cookie tray special while saving time with these easy no-bake bars. The sprinkles and vanilla-flavor candy coating give these sweet treats a tasty cake-batter flair. Pictured on page 31.

WHAT YOU NEED
- Nonstick cooking spray
- 8 oz. vanilla-flavor candy coating (almond bark), chopped
- ¼ cup butter
- 1 10-oz. bag tiny marshmallows
- 1 tsp. vanilla
- ½ tsp. almond extract
- 7 cups bite-size original or vanilla-flavor rice square cereal
- ½ cup rainbow nonpareil sprinkles
- ⅓ cup powdered sugar

WHAT YOU DO

1. Line a 13×9-inch baking pan with foil, extending foil over edges. Coat foil with cooking spray.

2. In a 4- to 6-qt. pot melt almond bark and butter over medium-low, stirring constantly. Add marshmallows, vanilla, and almond extract. Cook and stir until marshmallows melt and mixture is smooth. Remove from heat. Add cereal and sprinkles; fold until evenly coated. Pour cereal mixture into prepared pan; press evenly with the back of a greased spoon. Let stand at least 1 hour.

3. Use foil to lift out uncut bars. Cut into bars. Place powdered sugar in a large resealable plastic bag. Add bars, a few at a time, to bag; seal and shake to coat with powdered sugar. Makes 24 servings.

PALOMA BARS

Garnish bars with sugared zest like you would a citrusy Paloma cocktail.

WHAT YOU NEED
- 1   cup butter
- ½   cup powdered sugar
- 1   Tbsp. lime zest
- 2   cups all-purpose flour
- 1½ cups granulated sugar
- 2   Tbsp. grapefruit zest
- ½   cup grapefruit juice
- 2   Tbsp. tequila, Mezcal, or lime juice
- 3   eggs, lightly beaten
- 1   egg yolk
     Dash salt
     Flaky sea salt

WHAT YOU DO
1. In a small heavy saucepan heat butter over medium 8 to 10 minutes or until butter turns golden brown, stirring occasionally. Immediately pour butter into a large bowl; loosely cover and chill 45 minutes, stirring twice.

2. For crust, preheat oven to 350°F. Line a 13×9-inch baking pan with foil, extending foil over edges. Add powdered sugar to cooled browned butter; beat with a mixer on medium until blended. Beat in lime zest. Gradually add 1¾ cups of the flour, beating until just combined. Spread into bottom and ½-inch up sides of prepared pan; press firmly. Bake 20 to 25 minutes or until golden brown.

3. Meanwhile, for filling, in a medium bowl whisk together granulated sugar and the remaining ¼ cup flour. Stir in grapefruit zest, grapefruit juice, and tequila until sugar is dissolved. Add eggs, egg yolk, and the dash salt; whisk until well combined. Pour over hot crust.

4. Reduce oven to 300°F. Bake 25 minutes more or just until filling is set. Cool in pan on a wire rack. Use foil to lift out uncut bars. Cut into bars. Before serving, sprinkle with flaky salt and additional lime and/or grapefruit zest. Makes 24 servings.

To Store Layer bars between sheets of waxed paper in an airtight container. Store in the refrigerator up to 1 week.

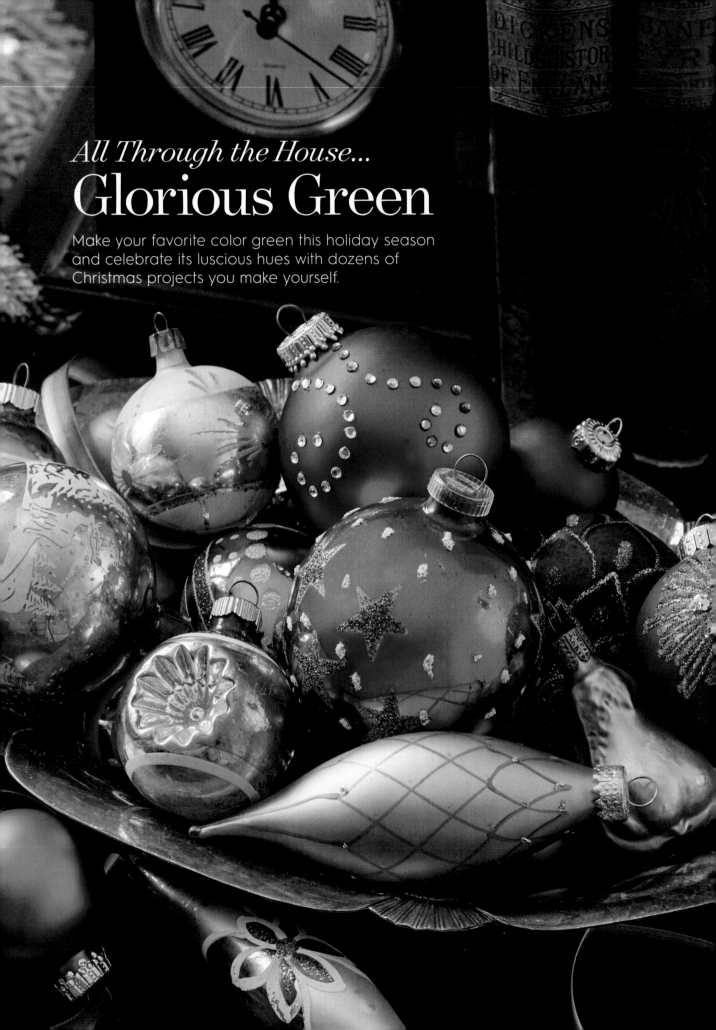

All Through the House...
Glorious Green

Make your favorite color green this holiday season and celebrate its luscious hues with dozens of Christmas projects you make yourself.

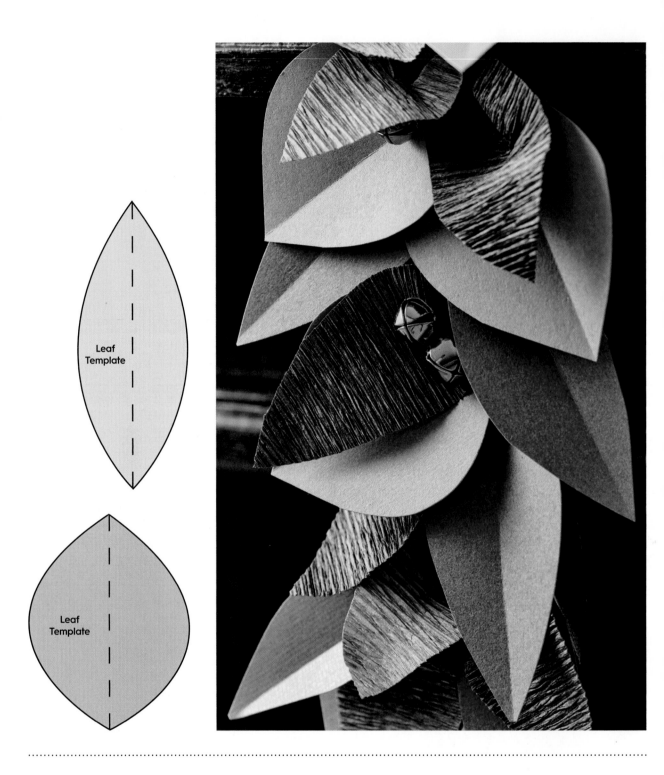

LEAFY-GREEN PAPER GARLAND

Dozens of leaf shapes layer together to make a textural garland of beautiful green leaves to display as a centerpiece or on a Christmas mantel.

WHAT YOU NEED

Crepe paper in shades of green • Cardstock in shades of green • String • Scissors • Hot-glue gun and glue sticks • Small green jingle bells

WHAT YOU DO

1. Using the patterns as guides, cut leaf shapes from crepe paper and cardstock. Cut about 50 leaves for a 3-foot string.

2. Leaving about 4 inches of string at each end of the string, use hot glue to attach one leaf at a time, alternating leaves from side to side.

3. Hot glue small jingle bells where desired.

BRIGHT AND SHINY TINSEL WREATH

Purchased green and silver tinsel garland wraps around a wreath form to make a quick and easy holiday wreath.

WHAT YOU NEED

Green and silver tinsel garland (about 6 feet of garland)
• Foam wreath form • Straight pins • Silver and green ribbon • Hot-glue gun and glue sticks

WHAT YOU DO

Starting at the top of the wreath, pin the end of the garland to the wreath. Wrap the tinsel around the wreath pushing the tinsel tightly together as you wind it around. Keep winding until the entire wreath is covered. Pin at the end. Tie a bow with ribbon and pin or hot-glue in place.

Swirls of paint resemble the look of Christmas evergreen trees all dressed in winter snow. Glittering white jingle bells on a string of ribbon add just the perfect touch for a holiday centerpiece.

PRETTY PATTERNED TREES

Use a clever marbleizing technique to create a forest of snowy green trees to set on your mantel or table.

WHAT YOU NEED

White cardstock • Acrylic paint in shades of green • Hot-glue gun and glue sticks • Scissors

WHAT YOU DO

1. For each tree, lay the white cardstock on a covered surface. Randomly squirt small dots of green paint in different hues on the paper. Make a squeegee by folding another piece of cardstock in half. Starting at one end of the paper, drag the squeegee through the paint, swirling back and forth until you reach the end of the paper. Let dry.
2. Enlarge the patterns, right. Trace around the template onto the patterned paper and cut out. Wrap into a cone and adhere with hot glue.

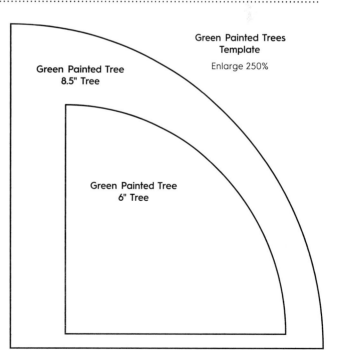

Green Painted Trees
Template

Enlarge 250%

Green Painted Tree
8.5" Tree

Green Painted Tree
6" Tree

GREEN ORNAMENT VIGNETTE

Vintage ornaments combine with newer baubles to create a lovely holiday vignette showcasing your love of the color green. Antique books with green spines stack up beside the collection of green-tone ornaments nestled in a tarnished silver bowl.

SHADES OF GREEN WELCOME

Natural and faux leaves and berries combine to make an elegant welcome for your front door.

WHAT YOU NEED

Artificial floral stems, leaves, and bouquets/garlands • Spray paint in a variety of green hues • Grapevine wreath • Wire snips • Foam wreath form • Hot-glue gun and glue sticks • Fresh greenery • Small green ornaments • Wire • Wire cutters • Narrow velvet ribbon • Wide ribbon for bow

WHAT YOU DO

1. Snip individual leaves and flowers from stems and bouquets choosing individual leaves and flowers.
2. Lay the leaves on a covered surface and spray-paint the pieces individually using a variety of green shades. Let dry. Attach the leaves to the wreath using hot glue. Let dry.
3. Add fresh greenery and wire in place. Wire in small green ornaments. Loop the narrow ribbon around the wreath for hanging. Tie a bow with the wider ribbon and attach with wire.

MODERN MIX

This beautiful green and white bouquet looks difficult, but it's made of only a few elements. We used green spider mums, white carnations, green hypericum, and Bells of Ireland. Create a grid with floral tape across the top of the container, then add water. Starting in the center, tuck cut stems into the vase, finishing with lower stems around the edges. Nestle green ornaments glued to floral picks to finish the festive look.

SPILLING SPLENDOR

Showcase white oriental lilies in a holiday arrangement with a glorious collection of winter greenery. Create a grid with floral tape across the top of the container, then add water. Position lilies sporadically around the center and base of the vase. Use greens such as bells of Ireland, eucalyptus, and short needle pine to tuck in around the sides to create a spilling-over-the-side effect.

FRONT & CENTER

Flameless candles illuminate this beautiful bloom-filled arrangement. Line a wood bread bowl with plastic wrap to make it waterproof. Create a grid with floral tape across the top of the container. Wrap base of flameless candles in plastic wrap to prevent moisture from getting inside. Position three candles, then tuck white hydrangea blooms, green mojito mini hydrangea, baby eucalyptus and white pine into the bowl. Add water.

STRAIGHT FROM THE WOODS

Venture out into the woods or to your local florist or grocer to forage beautiful greens for your winter arrangements. By using a variety of greens in different hues for your holiday decorating, the look will be inviting and professional looking.

Cedar Known for its wintry fragrance, this cut green can last up to two weeks indoors.

Scots Pine Nothing says holiday quite like pine—take some trimmings from a nearby tree to fill in and finish off your arrangement.

White Pine A common addition to holiday arrangements, white pine works great in swags and wreaths due to its soft branches.

Bells of Ireland These unique cuttings add height and a modern feel with meandering, chartreuse stems.

Cedar

Scots Pine

Bells of Ireland

White Pine

Eucalyptus Gunnii

Eucalyptus Gunnii One of the hardiest of eucalyptus, the long stems have a silvery color to add a touch of metallic to holiday arrangements.

Parvifolia Eucalyptus This small, delicate, fragrant foliage brings welcome texture to any arrangement.

Seeded Eucalyptus The sturdy, malleable stems of seeded eucalyptus work well when mixed with other flowers and greens.

Silver Dollar Eucalyptus With larger leaves than its eucalyptus cousins, these greens add lush fullness to your bouquet.

White Hypericum Similar to its red and green cousins, white hypericum berries are long-lasting and add texture to fill out an arrangement.

Variegated Pittosporum Technically a shrub, this variegated, rounded foliage helps fill gaps in arrangements with a double dose of green.

Parvifolia
Eucalyptus

Seeded
Eucalyptus

Silver Dollar
Eucalyptus

White
Hypericum

Variegated
Pittosporum

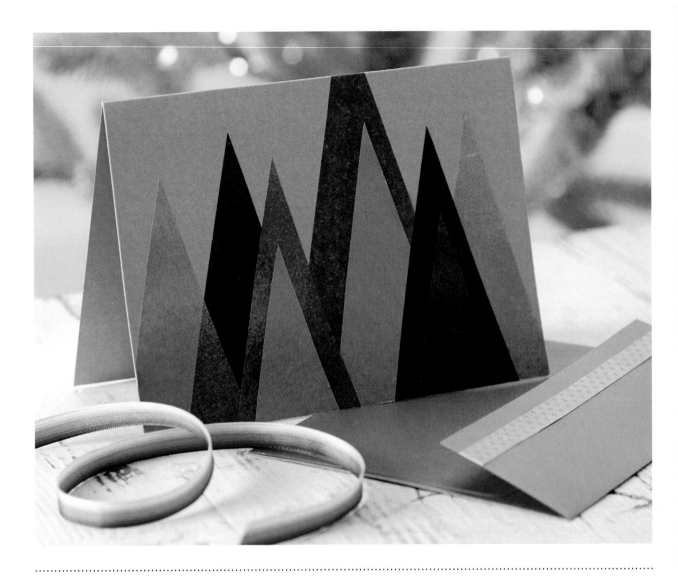

FOREST-OF-GREEN TREE CARD

Triangles of paper in greens and golds layer together to make a lovely paper forest of Christmas trees.

WHAT YOU NEED

Blank gold card (or create your own using gold cardstock)
• Tissue paper in assortment of green and gold colors
• Rotary blade, straight edge, or scissors • Spray adhesive • Narrow washi tape

WHAT YOU DO

1. Cut multiple triangles out of green tissue paper to create tree shapes using a rotary blade, straight edge, or scissors. Lay trees on top of card to plan the design, layering as desired. Attach using spray adhesive. **Tip:** Adhere the trees to the front of the card and then trim the card bottom.
2. Copy and print out the inside verse and adhere to the inside of the card. Trim around the edge with narrow washi tape. Trim the edge of the envelope with washi tape if desired.

The sight of snowcapped evergreens,
and the scent of vanilla pine.
Bring rosy cheeks and tingling toes,
and footsteps crunching through the snow.

Wishing you a warm, cozy,
and happy holiday season.

JESTER COLOR-BLOCKED PILLOW

Take advantage of the beautiful shades of green velveteen fabric available at the fabric store to make these jester-style pillows for your holiday home.

WHAT YOU NEED
Velveteen fabric in various shades of green • Sewing machine • 12×20-inch pillow form • Small gold jingle bells • Scissors • Thread to match fabrics

WHAT YOU DO
1. For each pillow, cut the following: choose one shade of green and cut a 21×13-inch back. For the front, cut two 11×13-inch pieces from two other shades of green.
2. With right sides together, stitch the two shades of green for front together on one side. Unfold. Put right sides together of this piece with the green back. Sew around perimeter using ½-inch seam allowance, leaving an opening to reverse pillow. Reverse pillow, put pillow form inside, and hand-stitch closed. Sew tiny jingle bells at the corners of the pillows.

JADEITE DELIGHT

Jadeite, the opaque glass introduced in the 1940s, was designed with color in its favor. Its green hue naturally fits all seasons and blends with accent colors—in this case, chocolate brown. A luxurious velvet ribbon weaves through the centerpiece, where an assembly of jadeite and tarnished silver vessels casually contain Christmas balls and sprigs of rosemary on a silver tray. The ribbon makes its grand appearance wrapped around jadeite and brown transferware plates and tied into a bow.

ALL-IN-GREEN TABLE SETTING

Gather your favorite dishes in shades of green and combine them with sweet Christmas candies for a stunning holiday table setting. A vintage green sherbet dish hold green gumdrops, a green mug offers hot chocolate, and a tree lollipop is the giveaway treat.

NATURALLY TEXTURED

The lovely texture of a simple cabbage leaf becomes a vase wrap to catch the light and hide unsightly stems in your glass vessel. Carefully remove the outer leaves from the cabbage, wrap around the vase, and tie with twine. Arrange the vases on a silver tray and add blooms, greenery, and vintage green ornaments.

SEA OF GREENS

A modern take on holiday arrangements, this woodsy gathering of green, leggy stems and naturals creates a free-flowing combo. Create a grid with floral tape across the top of the container, then add water. Add eucalyptus and berries and fill with pom athos and variegated pittosporum. Drill a hole in the core of the pinecones and glue in flower stakes to secure into the arrangement.

Shining Bright...
Star of Wonder

A single holiday motif tells the story of Christmas—let the brilliance of that star tell your Christmas story.

GALAXY OF VELVET STARS

Simply folded stars are covered with soft velveteen to create stunning Christmas ornaments or trims to tuck into your holiday decorating.

WHAT YOU NEED

Red cardstock • Red velvet or velvet-like fabric • Spray adhesive suitable for fabric • Scissors or rotary cutter • Hot-glue gun and glue sticks • Adhesive rhinestone stickers

WHAT YOU DO

1. Cut the fabric into 8×8-inch squares. Cut the cardstock to fit the fabric. Apply a generous amount of spray adhesive to the cardstock and adhere it to the wrong side of the fabric. Let dry completely.

2. Cut the velvet-covered cardstock into 2-inch strips with a rotary cutter or scissors. Use the strips to cut the shapes from the template, below.

3. Trace the templates, below, and cut out. The template will come just to the edge of the strip. (Each template pattern will make one section of the star.) For each star, cut 5 from the Star Ornament Template. Fold along dotted lines, first in half (outside corner to outside corner). Unfold. Then fold each outside corner to the center. Unfold. Fold into a triangle, overlapping the two corners. Secure with a dot of hot glue.

4. Cut one base from template. Using a hot-glue gun, attach the 5 star points to the base creating the star. Adhere a rhinestone sticker to the center of the star. Add ribbon hanger if desired.

**Star Ornament Template
(Star Points)**

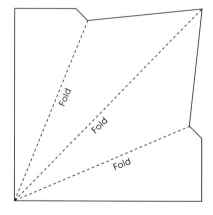

Fold

Fold

Fold

**Star Ornament Template
(Base)**

TRIO OF HOOP STARS

Glittering stars hang effortlessly in hoops of gold that seem inspired by the heavens.

WHAT YOU NEED

8-inch and 6-inch metal hoops • Gold or rose gold spray paint • Scissors • Glitter craft foam • Thin gold string • Hot-glue gun and glue sticks

WHAT YOU DO

1. Spray-paint hoops with gold or rose gold paint. Let dry. Referring to the templates, right, cut star shapes from craft foam. Cut on dashed lines and slide two stars into each other.
2. Hot-glue a piece of string onto the top of the star and tie at the top of the hoop to hang. Adjust as needed.

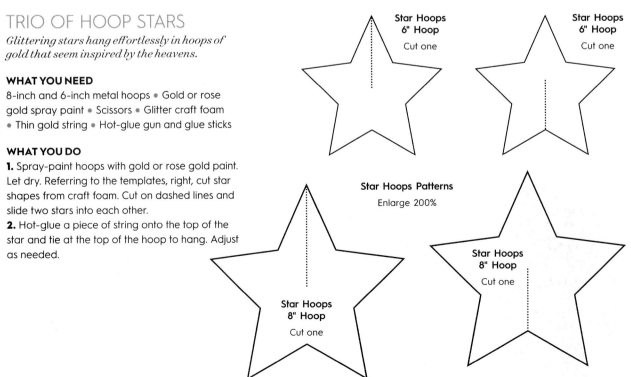

Star Hoops
6" Hoop
Cut one

Star Hoops
6" Hoop
Cut one

Star Hoops Patterns
Enlarge 200%

Star Hoops
8" Hoop
Cut one

Star Hoops
8" Hoop
Cut one

GOLD STAR SNOWBALLS
Wool dryer balls become the canvas for pretty embroidered stars to shine.

WHAT YOU NEED
Wool dryer balls • Embroidery floss in desired colors
• Embroidery needle • Pencil

WHAT YOU DO
Using a pencil, lightly sketch snowflakes on wool dryer balls. Backstitch along the pencil lines with the desired color of embroidery floss. Embroider all snowflakes in a single color or choose complementary colors. Stitch a length of floss to each ball and knot the ends to make a hanging loop.

STAR STRUCK

Let the stars in your life know how brightly they shine with a showy gift of gold.

WHAT YOU NEED

Wrapped package in black and gold print • Gold ribbon • Crafts glue • Purchased gold medallion star • Small piece of silver tinsel • Scissors

WHAT YOU DO

Lay the package on a flat surface and crisscross the gold ribbon, wrapping it behind the package. Glue in place. Glue the medallion where the ribbons crossed. Glue a small piece of tinsel in the middle. Let dry.

TWINKLE GARLAND

Simple cardstock takes on a new light when pierced and embellished with twinkling Christmas-tree lights.

WHAT YOU NEED
Metallic gold and copper cardstock • Scissors
• Crafts glue • Battery-operated fairy lights
• Double-stick tape

WHAT YOU DO
1. Referring to the template, below and right, cut star shapes from cardstock. For the Small star, cut two and overlap to make one star.
2. For the Large star, cut one, cutting out small diamonds from the template. Glue the small diamonds onto the areas indicated by gray on template. Let dry.
3. Lay out the stars and thread the fairy lights through the holes of the stars or secure with small pieces of double-stick tape.

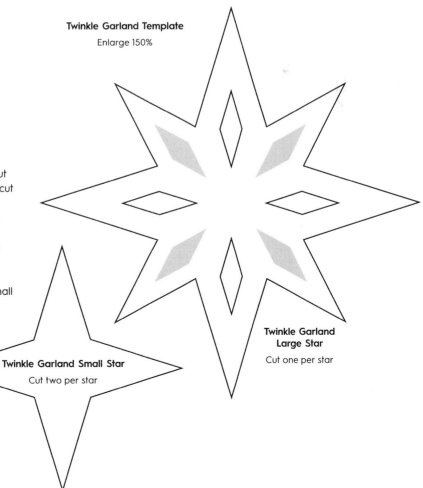

Twinkle Garland Template
Enlarge 150%

Twinkle Garland Large Star
Cut one per star

Twinkle Garland Small Star
Cut two per star

PAPERS WITH PRESENCE

An earthy collection of solid-color papers and coordinating ribbons in luxurious velvet sets the tone for these exciting handmade gift wraps. Create bold star stamps using a technique called linocut. Use a linoleum cutting tool to incise lines and cut away unwanted mass from a block of soft, smooth carving material. A wooden cutout, a stencil, or any drawing provides a good template. For a small package, we created a plaid tag with a very small brush and acrylic paint.

WHAT YOU NEED

Tracing paper • Desired template • Carve stamp block (see Sources, page 160) • Teaspoon • Linoleum cutting tool with No. 1, 2, and 5 tips • Utility knife • Quick-setting crafts glue • Wood scrap • Paint or ink pad • Solid-color paper

WHAT YOU DO

1. Place tracing paper over template and trace the design with a No. 2 pencil. Hold design firmly, pencil-side-down, on a stamp block and rub the back of a spoon over the design to transfer it.

2. With the cutting tool and a No. 1 or No. 2 tip, carve along each line (cut away from your body). Use a No. 5 tip to scoop out the material around the design. With a utility knife, trim excess material, leaving a ¼-inch border all around.

3. Use a quick-setting crafts glue to adhere your cutout to a thin square of wood that is slightly larger than your linocut shape. Once dry, press your stamp into paint or an ink pad, then press onto paper.

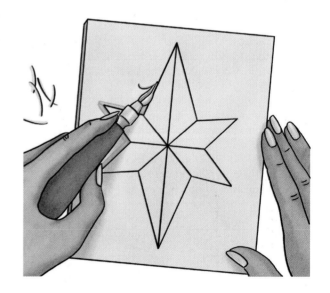

ALL THAT GLITTER WRAPS

Let the stars get in your eyes with these wraps that are sure to dazzle. For these stellar package wraps, think a simple palette of black, gold and white. Add a bit of curly ribbon or bakers twine to tie your galaxy together. For star templates, use cookie cutters or coloring book outlines as patterns. To create the layered look, cut shapes from specialty papers and glue smaller pieces on top of larger ones.

STAR-STUDDED TREE CANDLE

Cutout stars glitter with candlelight to celebrate the holiday season.

WHAT YOU NEED

Waxed paper or parchment paper • Air-dry clay • Rolling pin • Linen fabric or any other fabric with texture • Mini star cookie cutter • Drinking straw • 7-inch cardboard tree form (available at crafts stores) • Gold paint and paintbrush

WHAT YOU DO

1. Lay waxed paper or parchment paper on a work surface. Roll out the clay on the paper to approximately ¼-thick using a rolling pin. Use small star cookie cutters to cut star shapes in clay. Use the end of a drinking straw to punch small circle shapes in clay. To add texture, lay fabric on top of clay and gently press into clay using rolling pin.

2. Wrap the tree form with waxed paper. Trace the template below and cut out. Lay on the clay and cut out. Gently peel up the clay and wrap around cardboard tree form, pinching the ends where they connect. Let dry.

3. When dry, paint with gold paint. Let dry.

4. Set the tree on a plate or dish. Place a tea candle or non-flammable candle inside the tree.

Never leave a burning candle unattended.

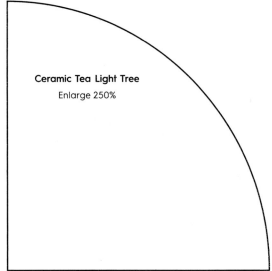

Ceramic Tea Light Tree
Enlarge 250%

SCENTED STAR SACHETS

Tiny little holes make stars that twinkle on these sweet gift sachets.

WHAT YOU NEED

Envelopes in desired colors • Transfer paper • Cardstock • T-pin • Quilt batting • Essential oil in desired fragrance

WHAT YOU DO

1. Trace the templates, right, and enlarge or reduce to fit envelope. Transfer the patterns onto the envelopes using transfer paper.

2. Place the cardstock inside the envelope. Using a T-pin, poke the holes where marked. Remove the cardstock and cut a piece of quilt batting to fit the envelope. Add a drop of essential oil to the batting. Place in the envelope.

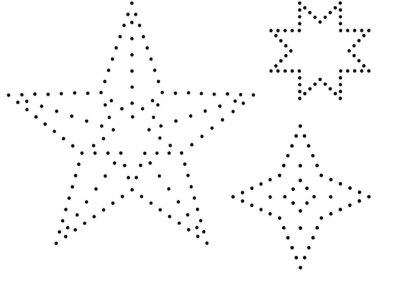

Nature's Inspiration...
Woodland Wonders

It's a beautiful sight when your home is filled with woodland decor that makes heaven and nature sing.

BE MERRY

CHRISTMAS CRITTER PACKAGES

Little treasures hidden in woodland creature boxes are sure to be favorite gifts for young and old alike.

WHAT YOU NEED

Gift boxes • Cardstock in brown, yellow, maroon, ivory • Scissors • Crafts glue • Paper punch • Red cording

WHAT YOU DO

1. Trace templates below, and cut out. Referring to the photos, cut out the shapes from cardstock using the appropriate template for each animal. Use a paper punch to make the eyes.

2. Arrange the pieces on top of the box and adhere with crafts glue. Let dry.

3. Add red cording if desired.

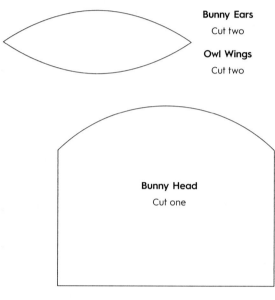

Bunny Ears
Cut two

Owl Wings
Cut two

Bunny Head
Cut one

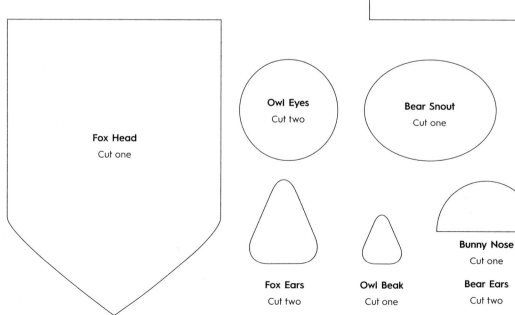

Fox Head
Cut one

Owl Eyes
Cut two

Bear Snout
Cut one

Bear Nose & Fox Nose
Cut one each

Fox Ears
Cut two

Owl Beak
Cut one

Bunny Nose
Cut one

Bear Ears
Cut two

MUSHROOM TREE ORNAMENTS

What fun to be inspired by the beautiful shapes of nature—just in time for Christmas.

WHAT YOU NEED

Recycled jar caps, variety of sizes • Molding clay (we used Crayola Modeling Clay) • Roller • Hot-glue gun and glue sticks • Acrylic crafts paint in red, orange, yellow, green, and brown • Paintbrush • Furniture wax • Decoupage medium such as Mod Podge • Glitter • Screw eye hooks

WHAT YOU DO

1. Use recycled jar caps in a variety of sizes as cookie cutters to cut out caps. Roll logs of clay to make 3- to 5-inch stems. Have fun with the clay by working with your fingers to add details like curves, twists, and imperfections in the stems and caps.

2. Air-dry overnight, then hot-glue the caps and stems together. Paint in shades of red, orange, yellow, and green, then dab on random touches of acrylic brown paint to create an organic effect on the stems and underside of the caps.

3. Rub with furniture wax to create imperfections, then brush tops with decoupage medium and sprinkle with glitter; let dry. Screw an eye hook into the top of each cap for hanging.

HUNT AND GATHER

From homespun hosting to delivering delightfully wrapped gifts, let woodland wonders create enchanting projects for your holiday decorating. Inspired by nature and made by you, most of the treasures for these thrifty trimmings can be found in your backyard. Find a favorite basket and gather pieces of greenery, berries, pinecones, twigs, moss, grasses, and more. Use these nature findings for many of the projects we share on the following pages.

EVERGREEN STAR WREATH

Make your own evergreen celestial greeting by putting together a heavenly star-shaped wreath.

WHAT YOU NEED

Fresh evergreens • Wooden or other star-shape form • Twine • Hot-glue gun and glue sticks • Heavy adhesive spray • Epsom salts • White glitter • Saw-toothed picture hanger

WHAT YOU DO

1. Cut evergreens to desired sizes to cover form. Wrap wooden star form arms and center with twine for a place to tuck in greenery or hot-glue greenery to star form. Hot-glue any loose parts. Cut extra evergreen pieces to size and hot-glue to fill in any holes.

2. Spray finished wreath with heavy adhesive, then sprinkle with Epsom salts and white glitter. Nail a saw-toothed hanger to the back of the wooden form.

SPRUCED-UP STOCKINGS

In the blink of an eye you can trim simple stockings with greenery bouquets. Pin on bouquets or weave sprigs of fragrant seasonal greens and favorites like reindeer moss, tallow berries, and hypericum berries.

WHAT YOU NEED

Ready-made stockings (we used red-and-white stripe and gingham option) • Hot-glue gun and glue sticks • ½ yard rug-hooking mesh fabric or ½ yard muslin • Safety pin • Tallow berries, cedar, reindeer moss, or other fresh greens and berries • Twine

WHAT YOU DO

1. Hot-glue or sew rug-hooking mesh or muslin the same size as the stocking cuff to the inside cuff seam and fold over the existing cuff.

2. Weave sprigs of greenery into the mesh or use a safety pin to attach a bouquet of fresh and fragrant naturals tied together with twine.

STAR/HAZELNUT GARLAND

Shine bright with a garland of twig and miniature hemlock pinecone stars tethered to a rope of hazelnuts. Hot-glue the hazelnuts and a sprinkling of eucalyptus onto florists wire and twine. Swap hazelnuts for whole almonds or try whole nutmeg for a spicy accent.

WHAT YOU NEED

Twigs • Twine • Miniature hemlock pinecones • Hot-glue gun and glue sticks • Gold acrylic crafts paint • Small paintbrush • Florists wire • Hazelnuts, whole almonds, or whole nutmeg • Sprigs of eucalyptus or fresh herbs

WHAT YOU DO

FOR THE STARS

Arrange twigs in simple starlike shapes and wrap centers tightly together with twine. Hot-glue miniature hemlock pinecones to the twigs; let dry. Gently apply gold acrylic paint to the pinecone tines' edges to lend shimmer.

FOR THE HAZELNUT GARLAND

Twist florists wire and twine to create a ropelike surface. Hot-glue hazelnuts onto wire-and-rope strand for a three-dimensional look. Glue in sprigs of greenery or fresh herbs where desired.

JOLLY WOODLAND ORNAMENTS

It's the best time of year to share good cheer. Dress up twig and cardboard shapes with miniature pinecones, moss, rose hips, berries, and other woodland finds. Garnish with eucalyptus leaves. Present them on a tray as take-home goodies or use as gift tags.

WHAT YOU NEED

Twigs or cardboard • Pinecone tines, reindeer moss, rose hips, freeze-dried cranberries, hypericum berries, eucalyptus, and other woodland finds • Hot-glue gun and glue sticks • Gold acrylic crafts paint • Paintbrush • Gold twine

WHAT YOU DO

1. Create your ornaments using a collection of twigs or cardboard shapes edged in pinecone tines, moss, freeze-dried cranberries, hypericum berries, rose hips, or other woodland finds. Connect the elements with hot glue.
2. For a little shimmer, lightly paint on thin gold highlights where desired. Glue gold twine loops to the back to hang as ornaments.

PINECONE FRAMES

Gather together in a new, old-fashioned way by crafting pinecone wreaths to display prized vintage photos that will bring a sentimental feeling.

WHAT YOU NEED
Cardboard • Purchased dried pinecones or found fresh pinecones • Needle-nose pliers • Hot-glue gun and glue sticks • Black-and-white copies of vintage photos • Gold twine

WHAT YOU DO
1. Cut cardboard into decorative shapes including circles, rectangles, and diamonds.
2. To dry fresh pinecones, lay on a screen for a week until the cones are fully open and tines are dry.
3. Pull tines off using sharp needle-nose pliers and sort into groups of similar size and color. Hot-glue tines in similar sizes and coloration to edge of cardboard shapes in an overlapping scale fashion.
4. Cut photocopies to fit frames and affix to cardboard. Glue gold twine loops to backs to hang.

PINE TOPS

Nestling a glass vase inside a larger vase is the secret to making this arrangement the center of attention. Set the small vase inside the larger one and fill the space between them with acorns and pinecones. Fill the inner vase with water and add pine branches or tree toppers to fill the vase. Set on a slab of wood and arrange a few pinecones on the surface.

3-TIER NATURE LOVER'S CENTERPIECE

Repurpose a curio accent table into a three-tier centerpiece (or look for a farmhouse-style, three-tier serving piece). Layer the surfaces with decorative spheres in a variety of sizes covered with freeze-dried cranberries, hypericum berries, and sheet moss. Place a few orbs on cut sections of birch logs to create different heights. Snuggle in reindeer moss, pinecones, acorns, and herbs. Display your arrangement on a kitchen island, hall table, or buffet where there's room to mix and mingle.

MAKE AN IMPRESSION

Nature-theme stamps give wrapping paper and clay gift tags a taste of the great outdoors. Cut a piece of matte white wrapping paper to desired size and spread out on a work surface. Using a rubber stamp and ink pad and starting with the lightest ink color, stamp randomly on the paper. Repeat with a second stamp and ink color, layering motifs as desired. An imperfect application gives papers a natural, fuss-free style. Embellish wrapped packages with ribbons, greenery, and do-it-yourself clay tags.

WHAT YOU NEED TO MAKE THE CLAY TAGS

White air-dry clay • Mat or parchment paper • Rolling pin • Natural or artificial greenery • Artificial berry sprig • Cookie cutters • Toothpick • Wire rack for drying • Acrylic crafts paint • Spotter and liner paintbrushes

WHAT YOU DO

1. Roll air-dry clay on a mat or parchment paper to about ¼ inch thick. Arrange greenery on the clay and roll over it to make an impression in the clay. Remove greenery.

2. Gently press faux berries into the clay in the desired areas. Use cookie cutters to cut out shapes and a toothpick to make a hole for hanging. Carefully lift the shapes and place on a wire rack to dry, turning several times over two to three days until clay is fully dry.

3. Paint ornaments using slightly watered-down acrylic crafts paint. To shorten drying time, place clay shapes on a parchment-lined baking sheet and put in a cold oven. Heat oven to 200°F and bake for 60 minutes. Remove from oven and let cool before removing from baking sheet.

ONE CHILL FOX

Bundled up from ears to toes, this cool fox prowls the snowy landscape. Easy patterns and embroidery turn felt into a fashion-forward forest fixture. The jute hanger complements the woodsy feel. Change the coat color and buttons to customize the ornament for your palette or your favorite hue.

WHAT YOU NEED

Non-woven felt such as National Nonwovens in teal, white, peach, and dark brown • Disappearing-ink marking pen • White, peach, black, teal embroidery floss • Two black seed beads • Small artists brush • Three mini white buttons • Jute • Crafts or fabric glue

WHAT YOU DO

1. Enlarge and trace patterns, below, onto white paper; cut out. Using a disappearing-ink marking pen, trace each shape onto appropriate felt color the number of times indicated on the patterns, referring to photos; cut out. **NOTE:** Cut the under body pieces from brown felt. **2.** Use two strands of embroidery floss for all embroidery unless otherwise indicated.

APPLIQUÉ AND EMBROIDER ORNAMENT

1. Using white floss and referring to photos, straight-stitch the jagged edge of the tail tip to one tail piece. Blanket-stitch the tail pieces together using peach floss. (For Stitch Diagrams, see page 158.)

2. Place the face on a body piece then place the coat on top. Adjust face to fit inside face opening of coat; remove coat. Using peach floss, straight-stitch outer edge of face to the body piece. Place the ears on the body piece, positioning short straight edge of each ear toward other ear. Using peach floss, blanket-stitch the ears to the body. **3.** Using the coat for placement, place the cheeks on the face; remove coat. Using white floss, use tiny straight stitches to join cheeks to face. Using one strand of black floss, stitch a bead to each cheek for an eye. Using black floss, straight-stitch a triangle between the cheek bottoms for a nose. **4.** Using teal floss and referring to photo, stitch large blanket stitches around the legs and feet, bringing stitches into center between legs and feet. Straight-stitch a vertical line through the center of the legs and feet. **5.** Straight-stitch the short edge of tail to back of coat near bottom. Pin coat to body. Using teal floss, blanket-stitch around coat edges and face opening. Stitch buttons to center of coat front using black floss. Fold a 6-inch piece of jute in half; glue ends inside top edge of fox. Let dry. **6.** Pin remaining body piece to back of fox. Whipstitch together using black floss, making sure to conceal stitches in the layers to prevent show-through to front.

Fox Patterns
Enlarge 125%

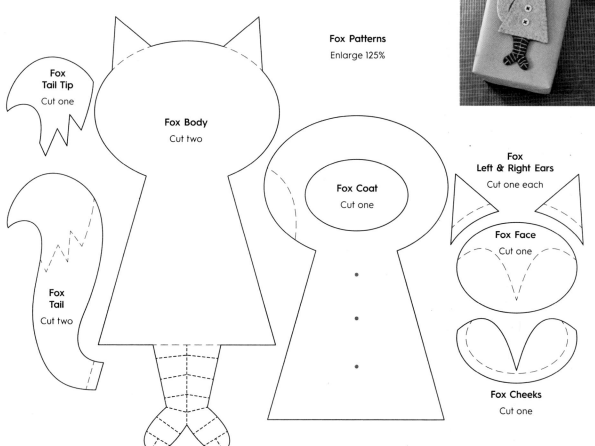

Fox
Tail Tip
Cut one

Fox Body
Cut two

Fox
Tail
Cut two

Fox Coat
Cut one

Fox
Left & Right Ears
Cut one each

Fox Face
Cut one

Fox Cheeks
Cut one

CITRUS CRAFTS

Making dried citrus slices is easy and you can use them for so many fun, nature-inspired projects.

WHAT YOU NEED TO MAKE THE DRIED CITRUS SLICES
2 medium blood oranges • 2 medium oranges or lemons • 2 or 3 clementines or 1 red grapefruit

WHAT YOU NEED TO MAKE THE GARLAND AND WRAPS
Cloves, bay leaves, greenery • Paper punch • Wood beads • Crafts paint • Cookie cutter • Dried citrus • Twine • Ribbon

WHAT YOU DO
1. Preheat oven to 200°F. Line a large baking sheet with parchment paper. Cut the fruit into ¼-inch slices. Arrange on prepared baking sheet. Bake 2 to 3 hours or until fruit is nearly dried, turning over once or twice if needed. Small fruit, such as the lemons and clementines, will dry more quickly (2 to 2½ hours) than the larger oranges. Cool completely (fruit slices will continue to dry as they cool).

FOR THE GARLAND
1. Press cloves into fruit near edges of dried citrus slices. Punch small holes into bay leaves using a paper punch. When making garland, wrap one end of twine, cord, or ribbon with tape (any kind will do). It will give you a stiff end for easier stringing.
2. String together on twine. Use a cookie cutter to punch stars from lemon and orange peels. String with dried citrus slices.
3. Paint wood beads with acrylic paint. String beads and dried citrus slices onto twine. Wrap garland with leaf ribbon.

FOR THE PACKAGE WRAPS
1. Attach a dried citrus slice and a handmade paper tag to package with ribbon. Wrap yarn around package and string through center of a dried citrus slice. Tie yarn around a eucalyptus sprig; trim excess.
2. String dried citrus slices onto twine and wrap twine around package. Tuck in cinnamon sticks.
3. Stack dried citrus slices and string onto twine or wire. Attach to pom-pom trim. Tuck rosemary sprigs into trim in wreath shape (use hot glue if necessary).

TREE SCENE

Outdoor touches give indoor dining a wintry alfresco vibe. The perfect backdrop for evergreen accents, wintry whites and warm wood finishes create a charming country Christmas scene that's easy to replicate. With an open mind and keen eye, your next stroll around the neighborhood may yield a treasure trove of gems from which to fashion these festive decorations.

GLITTERING GREENS

Let sparkly greens ground a seasonal tablescape like our candlelit grove of snowy trees. Line a work surface with waxed paper, then combine Epsom salt and glitter in a bowl. Use a foam brush to coat a variety of evergreens and pinecones with decoupage glue, then use a spoon to sprinkle the salt-and-glitter mixture. Let dry. For the Snow-Capped Evergreens, see the next page.

Set a beautiful woodland table with Snow-Capped Evergreen Trees for the main centerpiece. Then make Twig Napkin Rings to wrap around a linen napkin to rest on embellished white plates.

SNOW-CAPPED EVERGREEN TREE

WHAT YOU NEED

Preserved or dried leaves • Papier-mâché cone • Hot-glue gun and glue sticks • White spray paint (we used a semigloss finish)

WHAT YOU DO

1. Cut or pinch petioles from leaves. Starting at the bottom of the cone, position leaves, base at the top, and hot-glue to the cone. Repeat with additional leaves around bottom of cone, overlapping as needed.

2. Moving up the cone, add more rows of leaves, slightly overlapping until entire cone is covered. Create a peak at the top. In a well-ventilated area on a protected work surface, spray-paint trees and let dry. Add a second coat of paint if needed.

TWIG NAPKIN RINGS

WHAT YOU NEED

Cardboard paper towel tube • Jute twine • Hot-glue gun and glue sticks • Pruning shears • Found twigs • 220-grit sandpaper • Damp cloth • Crafts paintbrush • Decoupage medium • Extra-fine glitter

WHAT YOU DO

1. Cut cardboard tube into 1½-inch rings. Cut through one side of each ring to create a C shape. Wrap each shape in jute twine, securing ends with glue.

2. Cut twigs into 2-inch pieces, and sand to remove loose bark and residue. Wipe clean with a damp cloth and let dry. Hot-glue twigs over twine, covering half of the ring, opposite the opening. Paint twigs with decoupage medium and sprinkle with glitter. Let dry.

FABRIC GIFT WRAPS

Set the paper aside this year and choose eco-friendly and reusable textiles—tea towels, scarves, or cloth napkins can become part of the gift. Buy these items or make them from fabric remnants and no-sew adhesive hem tape. Fabric wraps also work wonders for oddly shaped gifts; simply roll the item up in the fabric and tie the ends with twine. Or place the fabric right side down and set the gift in the center before pulling fabric up and around the gift and tying at the top with a length of twine and a tag.

WHAT YOU NEED

Fabric, cloth napkins, scarves, or other textiles • Double-stick tape (optional) • Hot-glue gun and glue sticks • Greens, twigs, pinecones, or similar items • Cloth tape • Wood slices (buy online or cut your own) • Drill and small bit • Marker or paint pen • Natural cording or twine

WHAT YOU DO

1. For boxed gifts, place fabric right side down and set box diagonally in center. Wrap the bottom left-hand corner of fabric up and over the side of the box and hold.

2. Wrap the top right-hand corner over the box and hold (secure both corners to the box with double-stick tape if needed). On exposed sides of box, press fabric down the sides of the box while training folded edges of fabric to fold in a bit.

3. Pull ends of fabric up and over the top of the box and knot. Hot-glue pinecones to evergreen sprigs and secure under fabric knots using cloth tape.

4. Drill a small hole through wood slices, write a name or greeting on each slice, and tie to gifts using cording or twine.

INTO THE WOODS

Echoes of fairy-tale forests embellish an end-of-the-year tablescape that includes a green-and-white plate depicting a majestic buck on layers of coordinates and a deer ornament leaping across a partly rolled napkin. A woven place mat anchors the plates and swirl-handled flatware. Deer antler sheds overlap to form architecture for pinecones and Christmas balls that evoke a walk in the woods with holiday sparkle.

WITH THE GRAIN

Rustic moments emerge from slices of wood. Atop a charcuterie board, a bark-edged round is used as a charger and contrasts the dainty patterns of a green floral dinner plate and winter-themed salad plate. A smaller wood round slips over a napkin with a faux bois motif. Bottle-brush trees in ivory and silver are glued to slices of birch logs. Wood-handled flatware has a smooth finish.

KNIT BITS

Wool and cotton cable-knit sweaters are hallmarks of winter fashion. A rimmed bowl displays an iconic snowflake pattern; a mitten ornament warms flatware. An old sweater was cut to elevate the theme, with part of a sleeve rolled to fashion a napkin ring and cuffs stretched over pillar candles. Be certain candles are unlit or use flameless versions when candles are wrapped in fabric.

Oh What Fun...
Buttons and Bows

Buttons, vintage and new, combine with holiday ribbons and bows to make a Christmas that is merry and bright.

TINY BUTTON WREATHS

Colorful felt balls combine with mini buttons to make holiday wreaths to hang on your tree.

WHAT YOU NEED

Felted wool balls in desired colors • Small buttons in desired colors • Embroidery floss • Embroidery needle • Narrow ribbon

WHAT YOU DO

1. Plan the design by laying each button on the ball that it will be attached to. Thread the needle with embroidery floss and stitch buttons on balls. Then stitch balls together, sewing through the center of each ball. Tie in a knot at the end to form a circle.

2. Tie a bow with ribbon and attach to the top of the wreath.

CUTE AS A BUTTON

Large wooden discs transform into clever Christmas ornaments that look just like buttons.

WHAT YOU NEED

Circular wooden discs (See Sources, page 160) • Pencil • Drill and ⅛-inch drill bit • Fine sandpaper • Crafts paint in desired colors • Small foam brush • Painters tape • Yarn in desired colors • Yarn needle • Hot-glue gun and glue sticks

WHAT YOU DO

1. Lay discs on a table and use a pencil to mark where the four holes should be to resemble a button. Use a drill and drill bit to drill holes in the discs. Sand lightly and wipe off.

2. Use painters tape to block off half of the wooden circle. Paint half of circle using desired color of paint. Let dry. Use a needle and yarn to stitch through holes. Create a hanger with a small piece of yarn and glue to the back of the disc.

SPARKLING RINGS

Pipe cleaners and craft rings wrap up together to make mini Christmas wreaths with happy holiday bows.

WHAT YOU NEED

Metallic chenille pipe cleaners in desired colors • 2-inch wooden crafts rings • Felt in desired colors • Crafts glue

WHAT YOU DO

1. Twist one color of metallic pipe cleaners around a wooden ring until covered.
2. Cut felt into 5×½-inch, 5×⅜-inch, and 1×⅜- inch pieces.
3. For the tails of the bow, notch ends of the 5×½-inch piece. Fold piece to form a V; secure fold with glue, and glue to wreath.
4. For the bow, glue together ends of the 5×⅜-inch piece to form a loop. Press flat and pinch the middle with the remaining piece of felt; secure with glue. Glue bow to top of tails. Repeat with desired colors of metallic pipe cleaners and felt.

ELEGANT BUTTON CANDLES

Stylish velvet ribbon and silver buttons dress up candles for a glowing centerpiece.

WHAT YOU NEED

Purchased candles in glass votives • Shiny solid-color cardstock • Scissors • Pencil • Double-stick tape • Velvet and satin ribbons in desired color and width • Hot-glue gun and glue sticks • Silver buttons

WHAT YOU DO

1. Measure the circumference of the glass votive with the poured candle inside. Cut the cardstock to just wrap around the votive. Use double-stick tape to secure in back.
2. Cut the ribbons to wrap around the votives and secure with hot glue, layering as desired. Glue a silver button to the front of the candle atop the ribbon.

Never leave a burning candle unattended.

CHRISTMAS GREETINGS HOLDER

Extra large satin bows help display the Christmas greetings you love to share.

WHAT YOU NEED FOR TWO BOWS AND TAILS

4 yards of 4-inch-wide ribbon in desired color • Scissors • Fabric glue • 5 yards of narrow ribbon in matching color • Pencil • Ruler • Fine wire • Hot-glue gun and glue sticks

WHAT YOU DO

1. To make the large bows, for each bow, cut a 26-inch piece of wide ribbon and lay out on a flat surface. Bring both sides into the middle, overlapping slightly and glue in place using fabric glue. Cinch the middle and wrap another small piece of ribbon around the middle and glue in place. Let dry.

2. To make the tails, for each tail, cut a 36-inch length of wide ribbon. Lay it on a table, with right side up. Cut two 36-inch pieces of narrow ribbon and lay them on the wide ribbon about ½ inch from the edges. Use a ruler to measure every 6 or 8 inches, (or use the size of the cards you want to display as a guide) and mark with a pencil. Use fabric glue to secure the narrow ribbon at each pencil mark. Let dry.

3. Pinch the top of the tail and secure behind the bow using wire or hot glue.

4. Trim the bottoms of the tails.

MERRY CHRISTMAS

Button Ornament
Wrap

Flat Button
Wraps

Pink Bow
Wrap

Button Wreath
Trim

NOEL

Crisscross Trim

BUTTONS AND BOWS WRAPS

Vintage or new, satin or grosgrain, buttons and bows combine to make quick and clever wraps that are sure to bring smiles.

FOR THE BUTTON ORNAMENT WRAP
Remove ornament toppers from ornaments and glue to top of large buttons. Thread bakers twine through the tops and wrap to back of package. Add a bow and a sticker.

FOR THE FLAT BUTTON WRAPS
Thread a piece of twine or thread through the holes of the buttons and tie. Lay the ribbon on the packages as desired and glue the buttons on the ribbons or package using crafts glue.

FOR THE PINK BOW WRAP
Tie a bow and glue a special button in the center.

FOR THE BUTTON WREATH TRIM
Choose a square package and arrange shades of green buttons on the package in the shape of a wreath. Glue in place. Tie a bow and glue to the top of the wreath.

FOR THE CRISSCROSS TRIM
Thread four pieces of ribbon through an elastic hair tie at four points and pull to the back. Secure with tape or hot glue. Glue a button over the hair tie. Add a sprig of greenery under the button.

BOW KNOW-HOW

You have found the perfect gift for everyone on your Christmas list. Presenting the gift is just as much fun when you tie it up using the perfect bow. Whether you want to make a floral-style bow or a tailored variety, choose the ribbons that you love and then follow the steps to make the perfect bow.

TIERED BOW

WHAT YOU DO

1. Use three widths and three types of ribbon to fashion this bow. Cut the widest ribbon the longest, the narrowest ribbon the shortest, and the remaining ribbon a length in between. Notch the ends. Tie the stacked lengths in the center with another piece of ribbon, leaving long tails.

2. Trim and conceal the ribbon tails or use the tails to secure the bow to the package.

TAILORED BOW

WHAT YOU DO

1. Cut a piece of ribbon twice the desired length of the finished bow. Form the piece into a loop and secure ends with glue. Flatten the loop and secure in the center with glue. Cut another piece of ribbon and wrap it around the center.

2. Glue the ends of the wrapped center to the back of the finished bow.

TWO-TONE BOW

WHAT YOU DO

1. Choose two ribbons—one wider than the other—for your bow. Cut both ribbons twice the desired length of the finished bow. Form the wider piece into a loop and secure with glue. Center and wrap the narrower piece around the first and secure.

2. Flatten the layered loop and secure in the center with glue. Cut another piece of the narrow ribbon; wrap and tie it around the center of the flattened loop.

3. Pull the tails of the wrapped ribbon tight, trim the ends, and secure on the back of the bow with glue.

DIOR BOW

WHAT YOU DO

1. Cut four pieces of ribbon in graduating lengths. Form the pieces into loops and secure with glue. Flatten and secure the three largest loops in the center with glue. Stack all four pieces, adhering them together in the center with glue.

2. If desired, cut another piece of ribbon. Wrap it around the center of the bow through the top loop. Trim and secure the ends of the wrapped ribbon on the back of the bow.

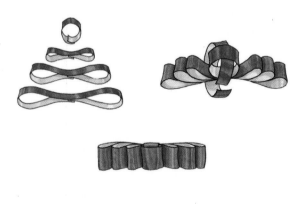

continued on next page

Tiered Bow

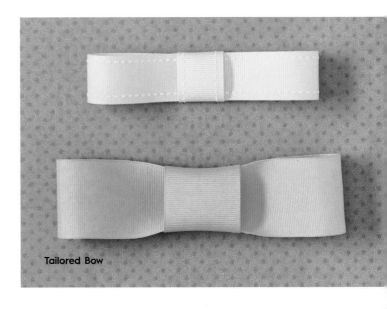

Tailored Bow

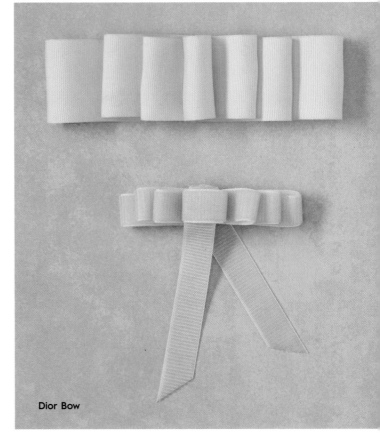

Dior Bow

Two-Tone Bow

What fun to wrap special gifts with beautiful ribbon. But it is the beautiful bow that is the center of attention on most gifts tucked under the Christmas tree. Choose the bow that suits your style and wrap it up!

continued from previous page ....

Classic Bow

Floral Bow

CLASSIC BOW

WHAT YOU DO

1. Being careful not to twist the ribbon, fold the ribbon length back and forth, forming two loops at the top and one loop in the bottom center. Start with a 2-foot length for an average bow.

2. Cross the top left loop over the top right loop.

3. Fold the left loop down behind the right loop and then through the bottom loop.

4. Pull the top loops taut, forming a knot in the center of the bow. Trim the tails and notch the ends.

FLORAL BOW

WHAT YOU DO

1. Determine the tail length for your bow and twist the ribbon at this point, keeping the right side of the ribbon facing you.

2. Make a loop and give the ribbon a twist. Holding the twist between your thumb and index finger, make a second loop the same size in the opposite direction. Twist the loop toward you.

3. Continue making same-size loops in this way until the bow has the fullness you want. Wrap a narrow width of ribbon around the bow center tying the tails together in the back of the bow. Do not trim the narrow ribbon tails.

4. Arrange the loops as desired to shape your bow. Use the narrow ribbon tails to attach the bow to your package.

TIE ONE ON

Choose patterned ribbons in similar widths to make a stunning package wrap. First wrap the ribbons around the box and secure in the back. Then, make bows and glue to the center of each ribbon.

WHO'S GOT THE BUTTON?

A button motif becomes the center of attention on a quick-to-make wrapping paper for the holidays.

WHAT YOU NEED

Small piece of crafts foam • Paper punch • Wooden block • Crafts glue • Crafts paint • Paper plate • Paper towels • White kraft paper • Straightedge or ruler

WHAT YOU DO

1. To create the stamp, cut a 2-inch circle from a piece of crafts foam. Create holes in the button shape using a paper punch. Glue the button shape onto a wooden block to create the base of the stamp. Let dry. **TIP:** Make multiple stamps so you can use many colors of paint without washing the stamp between times.

2. To create the patterned paper, spread crafts paint onto a paper plate. Dip the stamp into paint and stamp once on paper towel to remove excess paint. Then stamp onto the white kraft paper. **TIP:** Use a straight edge or ruler to make sure rows are even. Let dry.

BUTTONS-AND-BOWS GARLAND

A length of red-and-white bakers twine holds tiny buttons and bows for a sweet garland.

WHAT YOU NEED

Red and white buttons with holes • Red and white bakers twine • Needle • Narrow ribbon

WHAT YOU DO

Plan the design of the garland by laying out the twine and the buttons and bows where they will be placed. Thread the needle and go in and out of the holes on the buttons, arranging them as desired. After they are in place, tie the ribbons around the twine into bows.

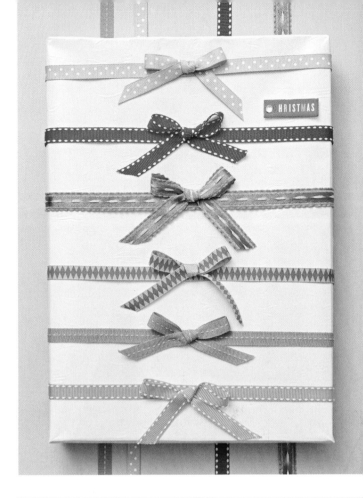

Full of Christmas Cheer...
Jolly Santas
and Snowmen

The Old Elf himself joins up with Friendly Frosty to
make projects filled with Christmas fun.

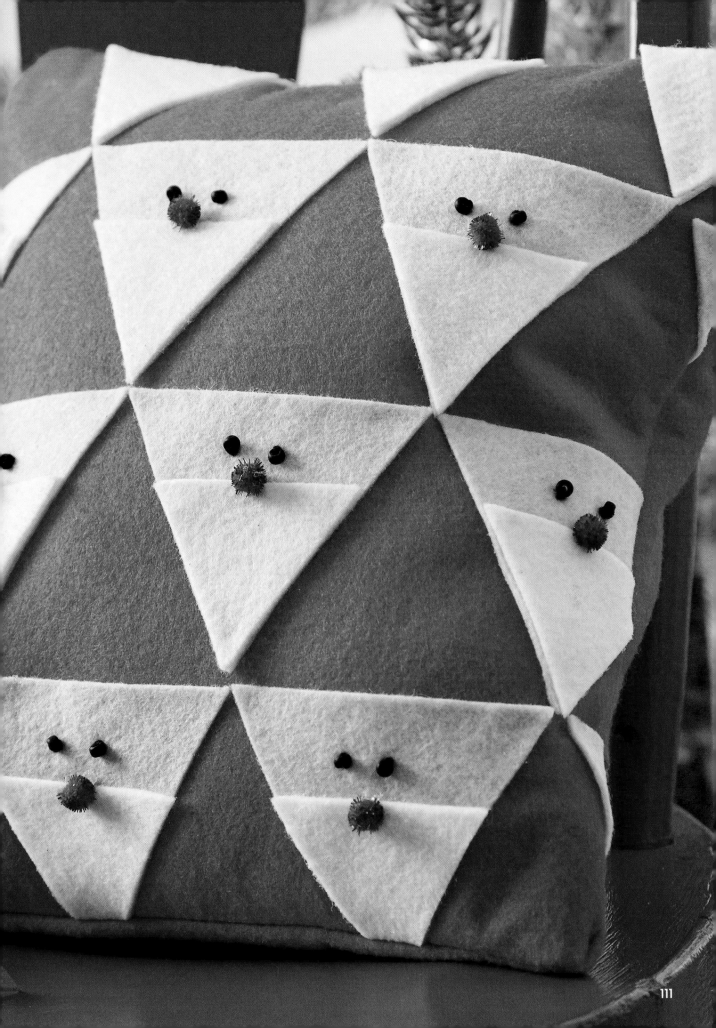

FROSTY HAND-STAMPED PAPERS

Grab some crafts foam and paint and start stamping handmade wrapping paper and cards using your favorite Christmas motifs.

WHAT YOU NEED

Foam craft sheets • Crafts knife and cutting mat or sharp scissors • Hot-glue gun and glue sticks • Kraft paper • Wood discs • Crafts paint • Disposable plate • Pencil with eraser

WHAT YOU DO

1. Trace desired design onto crafts foam. Use a crafts knife or sharp scissors to cut out. Hot-glue foam to wood discs to make the stamps. To make a background rectangular shape, cut a piece of crafts foam to desired size and hot-glue to the disc.

2. On a protected surface, place small amount of paint onto the plate and spread out to a thin consistency. Dip the shape into the paint and stamp onto the paper or card. If you want the rectangular shape behind the motif, stamp it first and let dry. Then stamp the motif over it. Let dry. Add eyes for the snowman by dipping the eraser of a pencil in the paint and stamping where the eyes should be. Add a nose by cutting a tiny piece of foam and stamping in place. Let dry. Use as wrapping paper or make into cards.

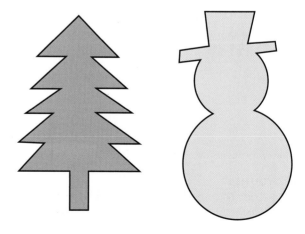

SNOWMAN GREETINGS
Scraps of cardstock and pieces of washi tape combine to make happy snowman cards to send to favorite friends.

WHAT YOU NEED
Black and orange cardstock • Scissors • White blank cards and envelopes • Crafts glue • Paper punch • Buttons • Washi tape

WHAT YOU DO
1. Cut eyes out of black cardstock using paper punch. Cut small triangles out of orange cardstock to create noses.
2. Lay white card onto a flat surface and arrange pieces referring to photo. Attach eyes, nose, and buttons to card using crafts glue. Wrap washi tape about two-thirds up from bottom of card to create scarf.

HERBAL SNOWMAN

Just like the old peddler with his Christmas pack, this aromatic snowman carries his own collection of goodies. Rosemary is draped over stick arms, and a necklace of anise adorns his neck.

WHAT YOU NEED

15×12-inch piece of muslin • Tracing paper • Water-erasable fabric marker • Polyester fiberfill • 13-inch-long stick • Tacky glue • Hot-glue gun and glue sticks • Small black buttons • Small black beads • Orange bakeable modeling clay such as Sculpey • Crafts knife • Thin string • 6×20-inch strip of wool flannel (scarf) • Scrap of green flannel (hat) • Whole anise seeds • Small sprig of rosemary

WHAT YOU DO

1. Enlarge patterns right, and trace onto tracing paper; cut out. Use fabric marker to draw around body pattern onto a double thickness of muslin. Trace mitten pattern two times on a double thickness of flannel. Cut out. Cut hat pattern from green flannel.

2. Sew around body outline adding ½-inch seam allowance, leaving open as marked on pattern. Trim body ¼ inch beyond stitching; clip curve. Cut 1¼-inch-long slit in neck back and turn body right side out. Stuff head with fiberfill. Insert stick through arm holes and stuff remainder of body. Whipstitch neck opening closed. Sew black beads on face for eyes and mouth.

3. Sew three buttons down the lower front section of snowman.

4. For carrot nose, roll orange clay into a ¼-inch-diameter ball. Shape into a ¾-inch-long carrot. Rotating carrot, score carrot-like ridges with a crafts knife. Cut the carrot top flat for ease in attaching to body. Make five more carrots from ⅜-inch-diameter balls of clay. Make hole with needle in each carrot top so they can be strung together after baking.

5. Bake clay carrots according to manufacturer's directions. Glue carrot nose to face. String remaining carrots onto 6 inches thin string, knotting between carrots. Set strung carrots aside.

6. Fringe ends of wool scarf. Wrap around snowman's neck, drape over stick and glue to secure.

7. Sew long sides of hat pieces together using ¼-inch seams; turn right side out. Glue to head; tack point to right side of head.

8. For mittens, with wrong sides together, stitch around mittens adding a ¼-inch seam, leaving the cuff opening unstitched. Knot one end of a 5-inch length of string through dots on each mitten pair. Set aside.

10. String whole anise seeds on thin thread. Tie thread to rosemary sprig.

11. Hang carrots, mittens, and rosemary on stick. Drape anise necklace around neck.

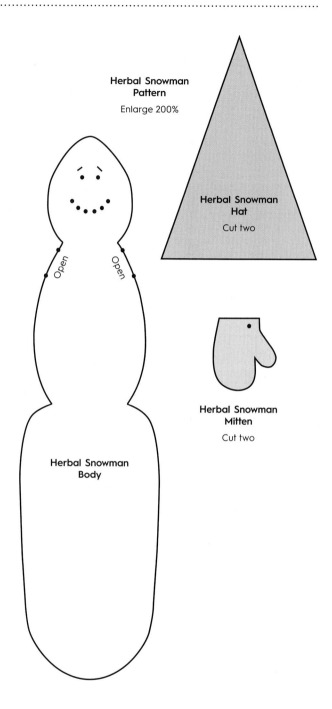

Herbal Snowman
Pattern

Enlarge 200%

Herbal Snowman
Hat

Cut two

Open   Open

Herbal Snowman
Body

Herbal Snowman
Mitten

Cut two

ST. NICK PILLOW

A simplified version of Santa is repeated over and over again to make the most delightful holiday pillow.

WHAT YOU NEED

½ yard red nonwoven felt such as National Nonwovens • ¼ yards each peach and white nonwoven felt such as National Nonwovens • Spray adhesive suitable for fabric • Small black beads • Black thread • Needle • Mini red pom poms • Hot-glue gun and glue sticks • Fiberfill batting

WHAT YOU DO

1. Cut two 13×13-inch pieces of red felt. Trace template, right. Cut 12 pieces from peach and 12 pieces from white.

2. Using spray adhesive, attach white pieces to peach as shown in photo. Sew black beads onto triangles for eyes. Using spray adhesive, attach peach triangles to red felt as shown in photo.

3. Place right sides of red felt together, faces inward, with other piece of red felt. Stitch around the outside using a ¼-inch seam allowance, leaving an opening to turn. Turn pillow right side out, fill with batting, and stitch closed. Attach red pom-poms for noses with hot glue.

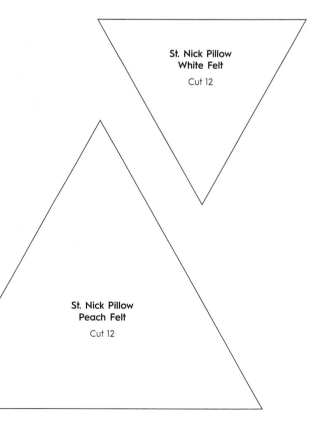

St. Nick Pillow
White Felt

Cut 12

St. Nick Pillow
Peach Felt

Cut 12

SANTAS VS. SNOWMEN TIC-TAC-TOE

Adorable little Santas and snowmen battle it out to see who can win this classic game perfect to play at holiday gatherings.

WHAT YOU NEED

Wood cones (See Sources, page 160) • Wood balls with flat bottoms (See Sources, page 160) • White and red crafts paint • Paint brush • Black paint pen • Scraps of yellow and orange nonwoven felt such as National Nonwovens • Mini white pom poms • Hot-glue gun and glue sticks • Small piece of white felt • Red washi tape

WHAT YOU DO

TO MAKE THE SANTAS

Paint a narrow white stripe around the base of the wooden cone to create a beard. Paint a red stripe and a white stripe around the top of the cone to create a hat. Make eyes by adding dots using a black paint pen. Attach mini white pom-poms on the top of the hat and as a nose.

TO MAKE THE SNOWMEN

1. Connect two balls together using hot glue, making sure the flat side is on the bottom. When dry, paint white. Create eyes using black paint pen. Cut a small triangle out of orange felt and use hot glue to attach for the nose. To make the scarf, cut a rectangle of yellow felt. Wrap around the middle and secure with a dab of hot glue. Let dry. Make five Santas and five Snowmen for the game.
2. To make the playing board, crisscross washi tape on a square piece of white felt.

COOL TRIO

Layered felt and simple trims make these little snowmen just too cute to melt.

WHAT YOU NEED

Dark red flannel • Small pieces of non-woven wool felt such as National Nonwovens or wool in off-white, orange, green, gold, green plaid • Orange, black, gold, green, blue embroidery floss • Embroidery and sewing needles • Tiny jingle bell • Sewing thread to match colors • Tiny red button • Polyester fiberfill • Antique gold acrylic paint • Artists brushes • 22-gauge wire • Wire cutters • Cosmetic blush

WHAT YOU DO

1. Trace patterns below, onto white paper; cut out. Trace each shape onto appropriate fabric color the number of times indicated on the patterns; cut out.
2. Using contrasting embroidery floss, blanket-stitch a face to each ornament front. Using orange floss, satin-stitch a nose or whipstitch a wool nose to each face. Using black floss, satin-stitch dots or stitch French knots for eyes and mouths. (For Stitch diagrams, see page 158.)

TO EMBELLISH ORNAMENTS

Ornament 1: Using gold floss, whipstitch a star to face and stitch a bell to center of star.
Ornament 2: Attach leaves to face, using green floss and running stitches down centers of leaves. Stitch a tiny red button between the leaves.
Ornament 3: Using green floss, whipstitch green plaid scarf around bottom of face. Fringe scarf.

FINISH ORNAMENTS

1. Stitch ornament fronts to ornament backs with right sides together, leaving an opening in bottom of each ornament as indicated on pattern. Turn ornaments right side out, stuff with polyester fiberfill, and hand-stitch openings closed.
2. Paint each ornament top with antique gold paint; let dry. Poke one end of a 12-inch length of wire about 2 inches into top of each ornament. Wrap remainder of wire around each ornament top, forming a hanging loop; twist wire together to secure.
3. Brush cheeks with cosmetic blush.

Snowman Face #1
Cut one

Snowman Face #2
Cut one

Ornament Background
Cut six

OPEN

Cool Trio Patterns

Enlarge 150%

Snowman Face #3
Cut one

Nose
Cut two

Star
Cut one

Leaves
Cut two

Scarf
Cut one

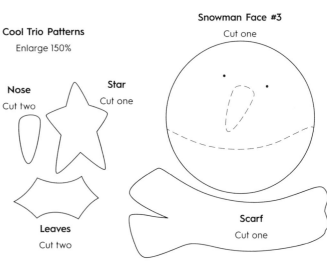

BOTTLE-BRUSH SANTA

When a bottle-brush tree nestles in a wooden egg cup, a surprising character begins to emerge. This tiny Santa will crack you up with simple assembly and extra-large versatility. You'll find dozens of places to display him.

WHAT YOU NEED

2-inch wooden egg cup • Acrylic paint in desired flesh color, red, black, coral, light yellow, winter white • Artists brushes • Fabric glue • ¼-inch pom-pom; red or pink • Black fine-tip marking pen • Artists eraser • Clear acrylic spray finish: matte • White bumpy chenille stem • 4½- to 5-inch-tall bottle-brush tree: red • Hot-glue gun and glue sticks • 1-inch pom-pom: white or cream

WHAT YOU DO

1. Paint the outside of the egg cup with two coats of desired flesh color, letting dry after each coat.

2. Paint the egg cup base with two coats of red, letting dry after each coat.

3. Using fabric glue, adhere the ¼-inch pom-pom to egg cup for nose. Using a pencil and referring to the photo, draw ovals for eyes. Trace pencil lines with a black fine-tip marking pen. Erase any visible pencil lines. Paint eyes black. Paint nose and cheeks coral. Highlight the eyes with light yellow. Paint eyebrows winter white. Let dry. Apply acrylic spray finish all over egg cup; let dry.

4. Use fabric glue to adhere a 4-inch length of bumpy chenille stem to the egg cup, bending the piece around the face to make the beard. Trim, if necessary. Glue another 4-inch length of chenille stem around top back edge of egg cup for Santa's hair.

5. Hot-glue the bottle-brush tree inside the egg cup. Use fabric glue to attach the 1-inch pom-pom to top of bottle-brush tree; let dry.

TRIO OF SNOWMEN
TABLE RUNNER

*A family of snowmen make the coolest combination on a
winter blue table runner.*

WHAT YOU NEED

½ yard of lightweight fusible web • Scraps of light blue,
white, orange, blue, cream prints (appliqués) • ⅝ yard
of light blue print (appliqué foundations and binding)
- 18×21-inch piece (fat quarter) of white tone-on-tone fabric
- 18×21-inch piece (fat quarter) of cream tone-on-tone fabric
- Embroidery floss: colors to match appliqués and black
- 220-grit sandpaper • 18×47-inch rectangle of batting
- ¾ yard of backing fabric

WHAT YOU DO

FINISHED RUNNER:

12½×41½ inches

Yardages and cutting instructions are based on 42 inches
of usable fabric width. Measurements include ¼-inch
seam allowances. Sew with right sides together unless
otherwise stated.

CUT THE FABRICS

1. Enlarge patterns, opposite. Lay lightweight fusible web,
paper side up, over patterns. Use a pencil to trace each
pattern twice, leaving about ½ inch between tracings. Cut
out fusible web shapes roughly ¼ inch outside traced lines.
2. Following manufacturer's instructions, press fusible-web
shapes onto wrong side of appropriate fabric scraps; let
cool. Cut out shapes on drawn lines. Peel off paper backings.
From light blue print, cut:
2—12½×15½-inch rectangles
4—3⅞-inch squares
4—3½-inch squares
3—2½×42-inch binding strips
From white tone-on-tone fabric, cut:
4—3⅞-inch squares
From cream tone-on-tone fabric, cut:
4—3⅞-inch squares

APPLIQUÉ SNOWMAN BLOCKS

1. Referring to the Appliqué Placement Diagram, opposite,
arrange appliqué pieces on a 12½×15½-inch light blue print
rectangle; fuse pieces in place.
2. Use two strands of embroidery floss for all embroidery.
(For Stitch Diagrams, see page 158.)
3. Blanket-stitch around each piece using matching
embroidery floss. Using two strands of black floss, backstitch
the curved eyes. Use black to stitch French knots for dot eyes
and mouths. Use black to backstitch the earmuffs headband.
4. Repeat to make a second snowman block.

MAKE THE STAR BLOCK

The Star Block uses fat quarters, made with ¼ yard of fabric
cut to 18×21 inches. A fat quarter offers versatility as you
cut pieces.
1. Use a pencil to mark a diagonal line on wrong side of
each light blue print 3⅞-inch square. (To prevent fabric
from stretching as you draw lines, place 220-grit sandpaper
under each square.)
2. Layer a marked light blue print square atop a white or
cream tone-on-tone 3⅞-inch square. Sew together with two
seams, stitching ¼-inch on each side of drawn line (Triangle-
Square Diagram). Cut pair apart on drawn line; open and
press toward darker color to make two triangle-squares.
Each triangle-square should be 3½ inches square including
seam allowances. Using same fabrics, repeat to make eight
triangle-squares total (four blue-white and four blue-cream).
3. Use a pencil to mark a diagonal line on wrong side of
each remaining cream tone-on-tone print 3⅞-inch square.
(To prevent fabric from stretching as you draw lines, place
220-grit sandpaper under each square.)

4. Layer a marked cream tone-on-tone print square atop a white tone-on-tone 3⅞-inch square. Sew together with two seams, stitching ¼ inch on each side of drawn line (Triangle-Square Diagram). Cut pair apart on drawn line; open and press seam toward darker color to make two triangle-squares. Each triangle-square should be 3½ inches square including seam allowances. Using same fabrics, repeat to make four triangle-squares total.

5. Referring to the Star Block Diagram, right, lay out 12 triangle-squares and four light blue 3½-inch squares in four rows. Sew together pieces in each row; press seams open. Join rows to make a star block; press seams open. The block should be 12½ inches square.

ASSEMBLE THE QUILT TOP
Referring to photo, above, lay out blocks in a vertical row with star block in center. Sew together blocks to complete quilt top. Press seams in one direction.

FINISH QUILT
1. Layer quilt top, batting, and backing. Quilt as desired. Bind with light blue print binding strips.
2. Mix foundation and backing fabrics for unexpected contrast or use the same fabric for both to convey simple elegance.

3½" sq.

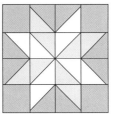

Star Block Diagram

3⅞" sq.

Triangle-Square Diagram

Appliqué Placement Diagram

1"   1¾"   1"

Snowman Patterns

Enlarge 250%

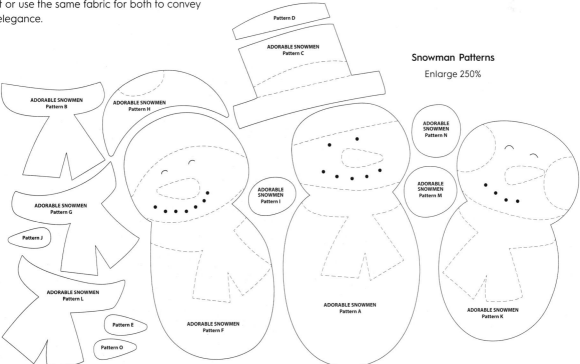

ADORABLE SNOWMEN
Pattern D

ADORABLE SNOWMEN
Pattern C

ADORABLE SNOWMEN
Pattern B

ADORABLE SNOWMEN
Pattern H

ADORABLE
SNOWMEN
Pattern N

ADORABLE
SNOWMEN
Pattern I

ADORABLE
SNOWMEN
Pattern M

ADORABLE SNOWMEN
Pattern G

Pattern J

ADORABLE SNOWMEN
Pattern L

Pattern E

Pattern O

ADORABLE SNOWMEN
Pattern F

ADORABLE SNOWMEN
Pattern A

ADORABLE SNOWMEN
Pattern K

Simple and Festive...

One-Pan Parties

From appetizers to desserts, one-pan dishes can ease the kitchen fuss and make serving a breeze at your holiday gatherings.

EASY SAUSAGE-PESTO RING

Basil pesto, Italian sausage, and mozzarella cheese star in this savory pull-apart bread recipe.

WHAT YOU NEED

5	Tbsp. butter, melted
2	16.3-oz. pkg. refrigerated biscuits (16 total)
⅓	cup purchased or homemade basil pesto
⅓	cup cooked and crumbled bulk Italian sausage (about 3 oz.)
1¼	cups shredded Italian cheese blend
	Chopped fresh basil or flat-leaf parsley (optional)

WHAT YOU DO

1. Preheat oven to 350°F. Grease a 10-inch fluted tube pan with 3 Tbsp. butter.

2. Top each biscuit with 1 tsp. pesto, 1 tsp. sausage, and 1 Tbsp. cheese. Stack 4 biscuits; press down gently. Turn stack on its side and place in pan. Repeat with remaining biscuits, arranging biscuit stacks in pan to create a ring. Drizzle with remaining 2 Tbsp. melted butter.

3. Bake 30 minutes. Sprinkle bread with remaining ¼ cup cheese. Cover with foil and bake 5 minutes more or until a toothpick comes out clean, top is golden brown, and cheese is melted. Cool in pan on a wire rack 10 minutes. Remove bread from pan. If desired, sprinkle with fresh basil. Serve warm. Makes 16 servings.

PARTY WINGS

Chicken wings are a party must! This appetizer stands out from the crowd with two different sauces.

WHAT YOU NEED

	Nonstick cooking spray
2	lb. uncooked chicken wings, tips removed, cut into 2 pieces each
1	Tbsp. vegetable oil
½	tsp. salt
¼	tsp. black pepper
1	recipe Coffee-Bourbon Barbecue Sauce or Asian Sauce
	Thinly sliced green onions (optional)

WHAT YOU DO

1. Preheat oven to 450°F. Line a 13×9-inch baking pan with foil; coat foil with cooking spray.

2. In a large bowl combine wings, oil, salt, and pepper; toss to coat. Arrange wings in an even layer in the prepared pan. Bake 20 minutes.

3. Meanwhile, prepare desired sauce. Using tongs, transfer wings to a large bowl; drain any liquid from baking pan. Add ⅓ cup sauce to partially baked wings; toss to coat. Return wings to pan. Bake 15 to 20 minutes or until tender and golden.

4. Transfer wings to a serving platter. Spoon remaining sauce over wings. If desired, sprinkle with green onions. Makes 6 servings.

Coffee-Bourbon Barbecue Sauce In a small saucepan bring ¼ cup water just to boiling. Stir in 1 Tbsp. instant espresso coffee powder until dissolved. Stir in ¾ cup barbecue sauce, 2 Tbsp. packed brown sugar, and 1 Tbsp. bourbon. Cook over medium until bubbly, stirring occasionally; reduce heat. Simmer, uncovered, 5 minutes. Stir in 1 Tbsp. butter until melted.

Asian Sauce In a small bowl combine ½ cup hoisin sauce, ¼ cup reduced-sodium soy sauce, 2 Tbsp. rice vinegar, and 2 tsp. sriracha sauce.

NACHOS MOLE

This quick-to-prepare mole sauce captures the flavor and richness of traditional mole in a fraction of the time. Pictured on page 122.

WHAT YOU NEED
- 1 recipe Fried Tortilla Chips or 5 cups purchased tortilla chips
- 1 16-oz. can refried beans
- 2 cups shredded cooked chicken, pork, or beef
- 1 cup Quick Mole Sauce
- 2 cups shredded Chihuahua cheese, queso Oaxaca, asadero cheese, or shredded Mexican-style four cheese blend (8 oz.)
  Toppings, such as guacamole, queso cheese dip, chopped tomato, sliced ripe olives, thinly sliced red onion wedges, thinly sliced radishes, crumbled Cotija cheese, Mexican crema or sour cream, fresh cilantro, sliced fresh jalapeño peppers, and/or additional Quick Mole Sauce

WHAT YOU DO
1. Preheat oven to 350°F. Arrange half the tortilla chips in 13×9-inch baking pan. Spoon half the refried beans in mounds over chips; top with half the meat. Drizzle with ½ cup Quick Mole Sauce. Sprinkle with half the cheese.
2. Bake 10 minutes or until cheese is melted. Remove from oven. Repeat layers. Bake 10 minutes more or until cheese is melted. Serve with desired toppers. Makes 6 servings.
Fried Tortilla Chips Line a large baking sheet with paper towels. In a large heavy skillet or pot heat about 1 inch vegetable oil (such as peanut or corn oil) over medium until 365°F. Meanwhile, cut eight 7- to 8-inch flour or corn tortillas into wedges. Add tortilla wedges to hot oil in small batches. Cook 1 to 2 minutes or until golden brown, turning once. Remove chips from oil with a slotted spoon; drain on paper towels. If desired, sprinkle lightly with coarse salt.
Quick Mole Sauce In large dry skillet over medium toast 2 Tbsp. pumpkin seeds and 2 tsp. sesame seeds 2 to 3 minutes or until toasted. Remove from skillet. In same skillet cook 1 cup chopped onion and 2 cloves garlic, minced, in 1 Tbsp. hot canola oil 3 minutes or until tender. Stir in 2 to 3 tsp. chili powder, ½ tsp. ground cumin, and ¼ tsp. ground cinnamon. Cook 1 minute more. Stir in 1 cup barbecue sauce, ½ oz. chopped bittersweet chocolate, and, if desired, hot pepper sauce to taste. Bring to boiling; reduce heat. Simmer until chocolate is melted. Cool slightly. Transfer onion mixture and toasted seeds to a blender or food processor. Cover and blend or process until smooth. Thin with water if needed; cool. Makes 1½ cups.

MEDJOOL DATE, PANCETTA, AND BLUE CHEESE MELT

This rich dip will become the hit of your appetizer buffet.

WHAT YOU NEED
- Nonstick cooking spray
- 4 oz. pancetta, finely chopped
- 1 shallot, thinly sliced
- ¾ cup chopped pitted Medjool dates
- 1 8-oz. pkg. cream cheese, softened
- ½ cup crumbled blue cheese
- ½ cup balsamic vinegar
- 2 Tbsp. packed brown sugar
- 2 Tbsp. chopped pecans, toasted
  Crackers, melba toast rounds, and/or fresh figs

WHAT YOU DO
1. Lightly coat a 1½-qt. round ceramic or glass baking dish with cooking spray; set aside. In a 6-qt. electric pressure cooker use the saute setting to cook pancetta 3 minutes. (For a stove-top cooker, cook directly in the pot over medium-high.) Add shallot; cook and stir 2 minutes more or until pancetta is crisp. Transfer to a medium bowl. Add dates, cream cheese, and blue cheese to pancetta; mix well. Spoon cheese mixture into prepared dish. Place a steam rack in pressure cooker. Add 1 cup water to pot. Cut three double-thick, 18×3-inch heavy foil strips. Crisscross strips and place dish on top of crisscross. Use foil strips to transfer dish to steam rack. Lock lid in place. Set electric cooker on high pressure to cook 10 minutes. (For stove-top cooker, bring up to pressure over medium-high; reduce heat enough to maintain steady pressure. Cook 10 minutes. Remove from heat.) For both models, release pressure quickly. Open lid carefully. Use foil strips to lift dish out of pot.
2. Meanwhile, in a small saucepan combine vinegar and brown sugar. Bring to boiling; reduce heat. Simmer, uncovered, 5 to 7 minutes or until reduced by half. Cool. Drizzle cheese melt with balsamic reduction. Sprinkle with pecans. Serve with crackers, melba toast rounds, and/or fresh figs. Makes 10 servings.

WINTER POTATO GRATIN

The combination of butternut squash and Yukon gold potatoes makes this scalloped-potatoes casserole colorful and craveable.

WHAT YOU NEED

1½ lb. Yukon gold potatoes, thinly sliced (about 5 cups)
1   1½-lb. butternut squash, peeled, halved, seeded, and thinly sliced crosswise
½   cup thinly sliced leek or green onions
1   Tbsp. chopped fresh sage
4   cloves garlic, minced
1   tsp. salt
½   tsp. ground nutmeg
¼   tsp. black pepper
2   cups shredded Fontina cheese (8 oz.)
1½ cups heavy cream
     Fresh sage leaves (optional)

WHAT YOU DO

1. Preheat oven to 350°F. Grease a 3-qt. rectangular baking dish. Layer half the sliced potatoes, half the butternut squash, and half the leek in the prepared dish. Sprinkle with half the sage, garlic, salt, nutmeg, and pepper. Sprinkle with half the cheese. Repeat layers. Pour cream over top. Cover tightly with foil.

2. Bake, covered, 1 hour 20 minutes. Uncover; bake 30 minutes more or until potatoes are tender when pierced with a fork and top is golden brown. If desired, top with fresh sage leaves. Let stand 15 minutes before serving. Makes 10 servings.

To Make Ahead Slice potatoes, butternut squash, and leeks. Submerge potatoes in a bowl of water; cover. Place squash and leeks in separate airtight containers; cover. Chill up to 24 hours. Drain potatoes well.

ROASTED TOMATO AND BREAD TOSS

Rustic olive or garlic bread also works well in this light tomato salad.

WHAT YOU NEED

6   cups cherry or grape tomatoes
6   cups torn baguette-style French bread or Italian bread
¼   cup olive oil
⅓   cup balsamic vinegar
½   cup garlic-stuffed green olives and/or pitted Kalamata or green olives
4   cloves garlic, minced
½   tsp. kosher salt
½   tsp. black pepper

WHAT YOU DO

1. Preheat oven to 400°F. Line a 15×10-inch baking pan with parchment paper. Place tomatoes in prepared pan. In a large bowl drizzle bread with half the oil; toss to coat. Transfer to another 15×10-inch baking pan.
2. Roast tomatoes and bread 20 to 25 minutes or until tomato skins begin to split and wrinkle and bread is lightly browned, stirring both once.
3. Meanwhile, in a small saucepan bring vinegar to boiling over medium. Boil gently, uncovered, 6 to 8 minutes or until reduced to 2 Tbsp., watching carefully at the end (vinegar will reduce quickly).
4. Toss bread and olives with tomatoes in pan. In a small bowl combine remaining oil, the garlic, salt, and pepper. Drizzle oil mixture and reduced vinegar over tomato mixture; toss to coat. Makes 8 servings.

SWEET-SPICY BARBECUE CHICKEN MELTS

Take advantage of a purchased deli chicken or leftover cooked chicken to speed up these party-ready sandwiches.

WHAT YOU NEED

12   3-inch sandwich rolls, split
6   Tbsp. melted butter
2   Tbsp. honey
1   Tbsp. Worcestershire sauce
½   tsp. freshly ground black pepper
1½   lb. skinless, boneless chicken breast halves, cooked and shredded
1   cup chopped fresh pineapple or canned pineapple, well drained
⅔   cup barbecue sauce
¼   cup chopped pickled jalapeño peppers
1½   cups shredded Monterey Jack cheese
      Sliced fresh jalapeño peppers (optional)

WHAT YOU DO

1. Preheat oven to 350°F. Arrange roll bottoms in a 13×9-inch baking pan or 3-qt. rectangular baking dish. For the drizzle, in a small bowl stir together butter, honey, Worcestershire sauce, and black pepper. Set aside.
2. For the filling, in a medium bowl combine chicken, pineapple, barbecue sauce, and pickled jalapeños. Spoon filling onto roll bottoms; top with cheese. Add roll tops. Spoon drizzle over sandwiches. Cover pan with foil. Bake 15 minutes. Remove foil; continue to bake 10 to 15 minutes more or until cheese is melted and roll tops are light brown. If desired, top sandwiches with fresh jalapeño slices. Makes 12 servings.

BAKED CAVATELLI

Saucy, cheesy, meaty. This ultimate comfort food pasta dish will be a crowd-pleaser. Pictured on page 123.

WHAT YOU NEED

8   oz. bulk Italian sausage, lean ground beef, or ground turkey
3½ cups dried cavatelli or gemelli pasta
2   14.5-oz. cans diced tomatoes with basil, garlic, and oregano, undrained
1   14.5-oz. can reduced-sodium chicken or vegetable broth
½   cup fresh basil or spinach leaves, torn (optional)
⅓   cup water
2   Tbsp. olive oil
3   cloves garlic, minced
¼   to ½ tsp. crushed red pepper
¼   tsp. kosher salt
2   cups shredded mozzarella cheese (8 oz.)

WHAT YOU DO

1. In a deep 10-inch oven-going skillet or a shallow Dutch oven cook sausage over medium-high until browned. Drain off fat. Stir in pasta, tomatoes, broth, spinach (if using), the water, oil, garlic, crushed red pepper, and salt. Bring to boiling; reduce heat. Simmer, covered, 15 minutes, stirring occasionally (pasta will not be tender).
2. Meanwhile, preheat oven to 400°F. Sprinkle pasta mixture with cheese. Bake, uncovered, 10 to 15 minutes or until pasta is tender and cheese is golden. If using, sprinkle with basil. Let stand 5 minutes before serving. Makes 6 servings.

CHILI-RUBBED BONE-IN STRIP STEAKS

Warm, rich spices, lemony tomatillos, and sweet peppers make an already sensational cut of beef into a Southwestern extravaganza. Choose tomatillos with firm flesh and dry, papery husks.

WHAT YOU NEED

1   Tbsp. olive oil
1   cup chopped onion
1   lb. fresh tomatillos, husked and coarsely chopped
4   cloves garlic, minced
1   Tbsp. packed brown sugar
2   tsp. chili powder or ground chipotle chile pepper
1   tsp. coarse salt
2   bone-in beef top loin (strip) steaks, cut 1½ inches thick and trimmed
    Nonstick cooking spray
2   medium avocados, halved, seeded, peeled, and chopped
¼   cup chopped fresh cilantro
1   Tbsp. red wine vinegar
1   fresh red jalapeño chile pepper, sliced (optional)

WHAT YOU DO

1. Preheat oven to 350°F. In a 10-inch cast-iron skillet heat oil over medium. Add onion; cook 5 minutes or until tender, stirring occasionally. Add tomatillos and garlic; cook, covered, 10 minutes, stirring occasionally. Cook, uncovered, 5 minutes more or until slightly thickened. Transfer to a bowl; cool.
2. Meanwhile, in a small bowl combine brown sugar, chili powder, and ½ tsp. of the salt. Rub mixture over steaks.
3. Wipe out skillet and coat with cooking spray; heat over medium-high. Add steaks; cook 10 minutes or until browned on both sides. Transfer to oven and bake 20 minutes for medium-rare (140°F). Cover and let stand 5 minutes.
4. Stir avocados, cilantro, vinegar, jalapeño pepper, and remaining ½ tsp. salt into tomatillo mixture. Serve with steaks. Makes 6 servings.

GRILLED ZUCCHINI PARMIGIANA

Layer slices of zucchini with mozzarella, Parmesan, and basil-infused bechamel for a vegetarian Italian dinner recipe that's similar to a mash-up of lasagna and eggplant Parmigiana.

WHAT YOU NEED

5 large zucchini (about 4 lb. total), ends trimmed and cut lengthwise into ½-inch-thick slices*
   Nonstick cooking spray
   Sea salt and black pepper
¼ cup unsalted butter
⅓ cup finely chopped spring onions or onion
3 Tbsp. all-purpose flour
2 cups whole milk or reduced-fat milk
2 Tbsp. finely chopped fresh basil
⅛ tsp. freshly grated nutmeg
8 oz. fresh mozzarella cheese, thinly sliced
1 cup freshly grated Parmesan cheese (2 oz.)
   Flaky sea salt

WHAT YOU DO

1. Lightly coat zucchini slices with cooking spray on one side; season with salt and pepper. Working in batches, grill zucchini on coated side, covered, over high 4 to 8 minutes or until char marks form. Set aside. Preheat oven to 375°F. Butter a 13×9-inch or 3-qt. rectangular baking dish.

2. For sauce, in a medium saucepan melt butter over medium. Add onions; cook 5 minutes or until softened. Add flour; cook about 3 minutes or until light golden brown, stirring constantly. Whisk in milk. Bring to boiling; reduce heat. Simmer 2 minutes, stirring often. Stir in basil, nutmeg, ½ tsp. sea salt, and ¼ tsp. pepper. Remove from heat.

3. Spread one-third of sauce in bottom of the prepared baking dish. Layer with one-third of the zucchini slices (grill marks up) and half each of the mozzarella and Parmesan; repeat layers. Top with remaining sauce and zucchini slices (grill marks up).

4. Bake, uncovered, 30 to 40 minutes or until bubbling and browned. Let stand 20 minutes. Top with additional fresh basil and flaky sea salt. Makes 6 servings.

*Tip You need zucchini that measure 9 inches long after trimming to cover the width of the baking dish.

TURKEY AND WILD RICE SOUP

Wild rice adds nuttiness and chewiness (and nutrition) to this hearty and satisfying soup.

WHAT YOU NEED

2 Tbsp. olive oil
3 cups chopped fresh cremini or button mushrooms
1 cup chopped carrots
1 cup chopped celery
½ cup chopped onion
¾ tsp. salt
¼ tsp. black pepper
2 Tbsp. all-purpose flour
4 cups low-sodium chicken broth
2 cups water
1 cup uncooked wild rice, rinsed and drained
1 cup chopped green beans
2½ cups shredded cooked turkey or chicken
2 cups whole milk
1 Tbsp. lemon juice
2 tsp. chopped fresh thyme or ½ tsp. dried thyme, crushed

WHAT YOU DO

1. In a 5- to 6-qt. Dutch oven heat oil over medium-high. Add mushrooms, carrots, celery, onion, salt, and pepper. Cook 6 minutes or until vegetables are softened and mushrooms start to release their liquid, stirring occasionally.

2. Sprinkle vegetables with flour. Cook and stir 1 minute or until vegetables are coated and start to brown. Add broth and the water. Cook 1 minute more, scraping up any crusty browned bits.

3. Stir in wild rice. Bring to boiling; reduce heat. Simmer, covered, 40 minutes, stirring occasionally. Stir in green beans. Simmer, covered, 10 minutes more or until rice and beans are tender. Add the turkey, milk, lemon juice, and thyme. Cook and stir until heated through. Makes 6 servings.

CHEESY BEER AND BACON SOUP

If you want indulgent soup to serve guests, you can't do any better than this easy, cheesy soup. As a bonus, it's ready in just 45 minutes.

WHAT YOU NEED

10	slices bacon, chopped
½	cup finely chopped onion
⅓	cup all-purpose flour
½	tsp. dry mustard or 1 Tbsp. Dijon mustard
½	tsp. dried thyme or oregano, crushed
2	14.5-oz. cans reduced-sodium chicken broth
2	cups frozen diced hash brown potatoes
1	12-oz. bottle beer (not dark)
1	cup heavy cream
1½	cups shredded sharp cheddar cheese (6 oz.), room temperature
1¼	cups shredded white cheddar cheese (5 oz.), room temperature
½	cup chopped green onions
	Toppers, such as hot pepper sauce and additional bacon, cheese, and green onions

WHAT YOU DO

1. In a 4-qt. Dutch oven cook bacon over medium until crisp. Drain on paper towels, reserving 3 Tbsp. drippings in pan. Add onion to reserved drippings; cook until onion is tender, stirring occasionally.

2. Stir in flour, mustard, and thyme (mixture will be thick). Add broth all at once. Cook and stir until bubbly. Stir in potatoes and beer. Bring to boiling; reduce heat. Simmer 5 minutes, stirring occasionally. Stir in cream; heat through.

3. Gradually add both cheeses, stirring after each addition until melted. Stir bacon and green onions into soup. If desired, serve with hot pepper sauce and additional bacon slices, cheese, and/or green onions. Makes 6 servings.

FROSTY S'MORES

This oversize version of the classic s'more is sure to satisfy everyone at your holiday party and can be made up to 1 month ahead.

WHAT YOU NEED
- 15 graham cracker squares
- 1 cup sliced almonds
- 2 Tbsp. sugar
- 6 Tbsp. butter, melted
- 1 qt. (4 cups) chocolate-almond or chocolate ice cream
- 1 cup hot fudge-flavor ice cream topping
- 1 qt. (4 cups) salted caramel or vanilla ice cream
- 1 13-oz. jar marshmallow creme
- 3 cups tiny marshmallows
- 1 cup miniature semisweet chocolate pieces

WHAT YOU DO
1. Preheat oven to 350°F. For crust, in a food processor combine graham crackers, almonds, and sugar. Cover and pulse until crackers are finely crushed. Add melted butter; cover and pulse until crumbs are moistened. Press mixture into the bottom of a 13×9-inch baking pan. Bake 10 to 12 minutes or until edges start to brown. Cool on a wire rack.
2. Place chocolate-almond ice cream in a large bowl and stir until softened and spreadable. Spread over graham cracker layer. Swirl fudge topping over chocolate-almond ice cream. Freeze about 1 hour or until ice cream is starting to firm.
3. Place salted caramel ice cream in a large bowl and stir until softened and spreadable. Spread salted caramel ice cream over chocolate and fudge layer. Cover and freeze overnight.

4. Preheat broiler. Quickly spread marshmallow creme over top of bars. Sprinkle with marshmallows and chocolate pieces.
5. Broil about 4 inches from the heat 30 to 60 seconds or just until marshmallows are golden. Using a knife that has been sprayed with nonstick cooking spray, cut bars into squares. Serve immediately. Cover and freeze to store. Makes 16 servings.
To Make Ahead Prepare as directed through Step 3. Cover with plastic wrap, then with heavy foil. Freeze up to 1 month. To serve, continue as directed in Step 4.
Tip Broiling the marshmallow topping goes quickly enough that the ice cream won't melt. If you have a crème brûlée torch, use it to toast the marshmallow creme instead.

BANANAS FOSTER BAKE

This baking pan dessert captures all the flavors of traditional bananas foster —no flambé required.

WHAT YOU NEED
- Nonstick cooking spray
- 1½ cups all-purpose flour
- 1 cup granulated sugar
- 1½ tsp. baking powder
- ½ tsp. salt
- ½ cup butter, melted
- ½ cup milk
- ¼ cup dark rum or milk
- 1 tsp. vanilla
- 4 medium bananas, peeled and sliced
- ½ cup raisins
- 1 cup rolled oats
- ¾ cup packed brown sugar
- ½ cup all-purpose flour
- ½ cup cold butter, cut up
- ½ cup chopped walnuts, pecans, or macadamia nuts
- Vanilla bean ice cream (optional)

WHAT YOU DO
1. Preheat oven to 375°F. Coat a 13×9-inch baking pan with cooking spray.
2. In a medium bowl stir together 1 cup of the flour, the granulated sugar, baking powder, and salt; add melted butter, milk, rum, and vanilla. Stir until smooth. Spread batter in prepared baking dish. Top with sliced bananas and raisins.
3. In a large bowl combine oats, brown sugar, and remaining ½ cup flour. Using a pastry blender, cut in the cold butter until mixture resembles coarse crumbs. Stir in nuts. Sprinkle crumb mixture over batter.
4. Bake 25 to 30 minutes or until browned and set. Cool 30 minutes before serving. If desired, serve with ice cream. Makes 12 servings.

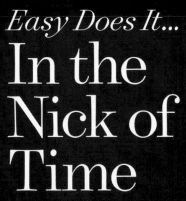

Easy Does It...
In the Nick of Time

Christmas is just around the corner, but in the blink of an eye you can make these simply jolly projects.

SIMPLE TRIMS

Nothing could be easier or more beautiful than these elegant ornaments you make in just a few minutes. Use purchased ornaments in colors that fit your holiday scheme. Then choose small-scale stickers with thin ribbons to match. Arrange the stickers in various patterns and thread the ribbon through the hanger.

VINTAGE TREE TOPPER CENTERPIECE

This elegant centerpiece requires just a few cut dowels to support the vintage tree toppers that stand all in a row.

WHAT YOU NEED

Vintage or new tree toppers with openings at the bottom
• Piece of ½-inch wood measuring about 4×16 inches
• Wood dowels small enough to fit into the hole at the bottom of the toppers • Saw • Drill and drill bit to match dowel size • Crafts or wood glue • Small piece of white tinsel

WHAT YOU DO

Plan the design by carefully placing the toppers in a row on the wood measuring where each will be placed. Mark with a pencil. Cut the dowels the length needed to fit each topper. Drill a hole in the bottom wood piece where the pencil marks have been made. Use crafts glue to glue the dowels into the holes. Let dry. Arrange the toppers by putting them over the dowels. Add the tinsel around the base of the toppers.

BOTTLE-BRUSH TREE FAVORS

Create a simple favor for your holiday table with golden bottle-brush trees and tiny terra-cotta pots. Wrap and glue a piece of ribbon around the top of the pot and let dry. Then "plant" a bottle-brush tree in the pot by securing it with some glue inside the pot. Write a name on the favor if you like.

SWEET CANS OF CANDY

*Small-size vegetable cans take on a new life when they are wrapped with scrapbook paper
and adorned with ribbon. Save those little cans, wash and dry them thoroughly, and glue
scrapbook paper around the outside, adding a scrap of ribbon if you like. Then fill them with
candy and other sweet holiday treats.*

JOYFUL HOLIDAY CARDS

Blank greeting cards become pieces of Christmas artwork when you adhere washi tape and stickers to the front of the card. Then stamp a Christmas greeting to finish the look.

LITTLE ARTIST GREETING

Let your budding artist help you design your holiday greetings this year. Create the design with markers, then reduce to the size card you desire. Add glitter to some areas of the card and make an envelope to match. Add a stamp and some love, and mail away!

POM-POM PLACE SETTING

Keep it simple this year with name cards that only take a few seconds to make. Use a small blank greeting card for the name card. Open it up and glue scraps of ribbon on the inside bottom. Glue a purchased or handmade pom-pom to the ribbon. Write each person's name on a piece of paper and glue to the inside top of the card.

CLEVER NOTEBOOK HOLDER

A single place mat becomes a much-loved notebook holder with just a few folds and some simple stitches. Lay the place mat on a flat surface and fold up the bottom third of the place mat. Stitch in place at the edges. Now fold the sides in to the middle and press. Stitch on the folds to make a firm crease. Put a purchased notebook in the fold opening inside. Close the holder and tack a small length of ribbon at the edges for tying.

PERFECT MATCH

Need a simple gift? Purchase a candle and using the color as inspiration, cut small pieces of scrapbook paper to fit the top of a small box of matches. Glue in place. Note: Paint sample colors are the perfect size to fit the boxes and come in any color you want. Add some holiday stickers or bits of ribbon to the top of the box and you have a striking gift.

PEPPERMINT PLACE CARDS

Candy canes stack together to make simply sweet holders for each guest at your table. Place four candy canes upside down and keep in place using a rubber band. Then wrap red cording around the top and bottom part of the straight areas and secure with hot glue. Remove the rubber band and adjust to hold name card.

FESTIVE FOLD-UPS

*Dress up your holiday table with clever napkin designs
that keep things stylishly simple.*

FOR THE NEUTRAL PLAID NAPKIN
Open up a square dinner napkin to lay flat. Bring the bottom
third up and crease the bottom. Fold both sides to the
middle then fold in half. Bring up bottom third to make a
pocket. Put flatware in the pocket and place on the plate.

FOR THE NAPKIN WITH STARS
Open up a square dinner napkin and bring two corners
together to make a triangle. Roll up the napkin and tie a knot
in the middle. Lay on the plate.

FOR THE RED PLAID NAPKIN
Fold a square dinner napkin in half, then in quarters. With
the open ends at the top, fold in half again lengthwise;
fold the open corner down to make a pocket. Place flatware
in the pocket.

FOR THE RED BOW
Open up a square dinner napkin and bring two corners
together to make a triangle. Roll up the napkin and flatten.
Fold both tails down, then crisscross in back. Use a piece of
ribbon to cinch in the bow. Lay on the plate.

SIMPLE SCARF STOCKING

Choose a soft fringed scarf and quickly transform it into a lovely stocking for Santa to fill with holiday goodies.

WHAT YOU NEED

Soft wool or acrylic scarf with fringe • Scissors • Thread in matching colors • Sewing machine

WHAT YOU DO

1. Enlarge and trace the pattern, right. Cut out. Fold the scarf in half, with the fringes at the top, right sides together. Lay the pattern on the folded fabric and cut two pieces, keeping the fringe at the top and being careful not to cut the fringe.
2. Sew around the edges using a ½-inch seam and keeping the top open. Turn and press. Fold the fringe to the outside, making a cuff. Cut a 1×6-inch piece of scarf fabric from the scraps and sew to the top for a hanger.

Scarf Stocking

Enlarge 150%
Cut 2, reversing 1

ADVENT JINGLE BELL TREE

A Scandinavian-style dowel tree becomes a charming Advent tree with jingle bells that signal each day. Purchase or construct a dowel tree. (See Sources, page 160.) Adhere small number stickers to 25 jingle bells. Loop a small piece of cording or ribbon through the bells and tie. Hang on the tree.

Wreaths of Joy...
Merry-Go-Rounds

Adorn your door with a fresh and festive wreath designed to greet your guests with a "Merry Christmas" welcome.

WINTER WHITES

A grapevine wreath layered with white berries, soft greens, and natural wooden snowflakes has the peaceful look of a snowy forest. Plump up the edge of a store-bought wreath with assorted branches found at crafts supply stores, securing with hot glue. White pip berries add density, but it's the glimmer of frosted berries and faux greens mixed with unpainted wooden snowflake ornaments, attached with brown stem wire, that define the look.

NATURALLY NEUTRAL

Sticks, corn husks, and nature findings are wired together to make a light and airy wreath worthy of a place on your door long after Christmas. Plan your design, overlap the sticks in a circle, and wire together. Then wire or hot-glue corn husk pieces, pinecones, and other nature findings to the wreath. Hang with a simple velvet ribbon loop or perch on a bench or mantel.

ALL THAT GLITTERS

Whether foraged from your yard or sourced at your local florist or crafts supply store, pinecones bring a little woodland magic to this easy-to-craft wreath. A flocked, faux evergreen wreath (no needles to clean up!) and pinecones sprinkled generously with blue and green glitter make this everlasting arrangement glow as if it has just been kissed by a Christmas Eve flurry of snow.

WHAT YOU NEED
50-75 pinecones • Florists wire • Decoupage medium • Foam brush or crafts paintbrush • Assorted glitter in greens and blues • Paper plate • Artificial flocked wreath

WHAT YOU DO
1. Wrap each pinecone at its base with florists wire. Brush pinecones with decoupage and sprinkle with glitter, holding cones over a plate. Let dry.
2. Fill wreath with pinecones, securing each with florists wire.

FELT FLORALS

The poinsettia is the holiday plant we all love. For an alluring alternative to the traditional version, we fashioned the iconic red bracts out of felt. The flower centers are tiny pink and red pom-poms for eye-catching contrast. Arrange them on a garland of eucalyptus leaves to add lush, everlasting greenery to your holiday decor.

WHAT YOU NEED

Nonwoven felt such as National Nonwovens • Florists wire • Wire snips • Hot-glue gun and glue sticks • Floral tape • Felt glue • Small pom-poms • Grapevine wreath • Eucalyptus garland

WHAT YOU DO

1. Enlarge and trace templates. To make five blossoms, trace onto felt cutting 30 each large, medium, and small felt bracts. Cut 30 each 6-inch and 3-inch pieces of wire.

2. Hot-glue a long wire piece to each large bract, positioning it so the wire centers on the leaf and hangs past the end 3 inches. Pinch bottom tip of felt around wire. Make a bouquet of six large leaves, keeping wire to back; use floral tape to bind stems. Shape bracts as needed.

3. Hot-glue six medium bracts onto large ones, staggering them between the large ones; set aside. Hot-glue a 3-inch wire piece to each small bract, this time leaving a 1-inch overhang. Make a bouquet of six small bracts. Hot-glue small bouquet to center of larger bouquet, bending stems as needed.

4. Use felt glue to secure about nine pom-poms to the plant center. Wrap wreath form with garland and use florists wire to secure. Secure the stems of each poinsettia to the wreath form.

Felt Florals Templates
Enlarge 200%

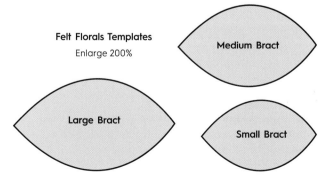

Medium Bract

Large Bract

Small Bract

HOOP DREAMS

Minimalist without being Grinch-like, this arrangement is ideal for homes with modern decor—and the instructions are equally as unfussy. If your holiday plans are more seashore than snowdrift, give this wreath a Christmas-at-the-beach look by using sand-color suede instead of red leather. Then spray-paint the evergreens silver or substitute branches of faux coral. Finally, paint the wooden balls shades of blue and green.

WHAT YOU NEED

18-inch and 12-inch flat crafts rings • Hot-glue gun and glue sticks • Faux leather cording in two colors • Assorted pine greens with pinecones • Wood crafts balls: ½-inch, ¾-inch, and 1½-inch • Red crafts paint • Paintbrush

WHAT YOU DO

1. Hot-glue two crafts rings together. Let dry. Wrap each ring with its own color of leather cording, overlapping the cording where the rings meet.

2. Arrange greenery in an asymmetrical composition, securing with hot glue. Paint half of the wood balls and leave others unpainted. Let dry. Place ball ornaments and secure with hot glue. Hang with lengths of leather cording.

THAT'S A WRAP

Crafting these decoupaged ornaments is the perfect project to use up that stash of scraps from old rolls of wrapping paper. Punctuate the arrangement with a scattering of faux berries from the botanical aisle in the crafts supply store. A candy-striped bow at the bottom is an exuberant finishing touch for this pretty-as-a-present faux boxwood wreath.

WHAT YOU NEED

Grapevine wreath • 18-20 faux boxwood sprigs • Floral clippers • Hot-glue gun and glue sticks • 12 white ornaments • Assorted wrapping papers • Decoupage medium • Foam brush • Waxed paper • Florists wire • Assorted faux berries

WHAT YOU DO

1. Trim bases from boxwood sprigs and arrange on wreath, securing with hot glue and overlapping sprigs until wreath form is covered.

2. Remove ornament hangers. Cut strips of paper approximately 1×4 inches. Brush decoupage medium onto a portion of ornament and the backside of one strip of paper. Press strip onto ornament from top to base, removing air bubbles, and brush on a top coat of decoupage. Repeat, overlapping strips. **Tip:** Paper half the ornament at one time, let dry, then finish second half. Lay ornaments on waxed paper to dry.

3. Once ornaments are dry, replace tops and use florists wire to secure ornaments to the wreath, mixing the order of papers and patterns. Tuck faux berries throughout the wreath.

POM-POM PRETTY

Remember the winter hat with a big, fluffy pom-pom that you loved as a child? Here, playful puffs of raffia ribbon give a nostalgic nod to that sweet snow-day memory, while a palette of green hues evokes the classic evergreen wreaths of yore. Buy extra pom-pom making forms and let eager crafters, young and old, help with the work.

WHAT YOU NEED

6-8 assorted green raffia ribbon spools • Waxed upholstery thread • 3⅜-inch pom-pom maker (large size) • Grapevine wreath • Hot-glue gun and glue sticks

WHAT YOU DO

1. Follow directions for pom-pom maker and create 50 to 60 poms in assorted colors. Use upholstery thread to tie off each pom-pom and trim poms to even out their shape.

2. Hot-glue pom-poms around the wreath into desired pattern. Arranging the pom-pom colors randomly rather than using a set color order adds to the playful look.

FRUIT AND FLORA

With its wide range of natural colors and textures, this botanical beauty looks as if you might have assembled the materials on a long walk in the woods, but you can source everything you need for this DIY door decoration online or at your local crafts supply store. Because all the elements are preserved or faux, the finished wreath will last for years. Just wrap it in acid-free tissue paper and protect it with bubble wrap, then enjoy for many Christmases to come.

WHAT YOU NEED

Artificial wreath with assorted evergreens • Faux hydrangea • Faux juniper • Faux eucalyptus picks • Florists wire • Dried thistle in red and lavender • Pinecones • Dried limes • Hot-glue gun and glue sticks

WHAT YOU DO

Start by arranging the largest elements—hydrangea, juniper, and eucalyptus picks—symmetrically and evenly spaced around the wreath. Secure these elements by tucking stems and picks into the wreath. If needed, wire each to the wreath frame. Next place thistle, pinecones and limes among and between the larger elements. Secure by wiring or hot-gluing in place.

PRETTY IN PAPER

When decorating is as easy as wrapping a gift, there's no reason not to deck the halls. Made of approximately 50 small party favor boxes found at crafts and party stores, this wreath takes little crafting prowess. Using leftover wrapping paper and coordinating scrapbook paper, wrap each tiny box, securing the edges with hot glue—it's much faster and neater than tape. The addition of festive gold cording immediately turns each box into a delicate gift, unifying the wreath's style. Layer the boxes onto a felt-wrapped wire frame with hot glue. Add a second layer to cover gaps and give the wreath dramatic dimension.

MIDAS TOUCH

Give a faux pine wreath a custom upgrade by adding greenery and a coat of festive gold paint. A generous layer of paint will begin the wreath's transformation. Coat an additional assortment of faux natural elements—such as magnolia leaves, pinecones, and berries—with the same gold hue. Mercury glass ornaments and other gold embellishments add just the right amount of shimmer. Wire in each additional decoration, beginning with magnolia leaves around the wreath's outer edge. If gold isn't your holiday color of choice, choose any metallic hue that suits you.

STITCH DIAGRAMS

Backstitch

Blanket Stitch

Buttonhole Stitch

Chain Stitch

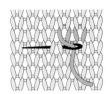

Duplicate Stitch

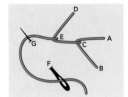

Feather Stitch

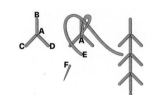

Fern Stitch

French Knot

Running Stitch

Star Stitch

Stem Stitch

Straight Stitch

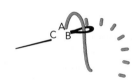

Whipstitch

KNITTING ABBREVIATIONS

BEG	begin(ning)
DEC	decrease
INC	increase
K	knit
LP	loop
M1	make one or to increase one
P	purl
SSK	slip, slip knit
TOG	together

CROCHET ABBREVIATIONS

BEG	begin(ning)
CH	chain
DC	double crochet
HDC	half double crochet
INC	increase
SC	single crochet
SL ST	slip stitch
ST(S)	stitch(es)

INDEX

A PROPER TABLE SETTING

When setting your dining table for the holidays, decide what dishes and flatware pieces are important for the meal you are serving. Use this guide to be sure your holiday table is beautifully set. The diagram shows where each piece should be placed. Adjust it as needed to fit your Christmas meal.

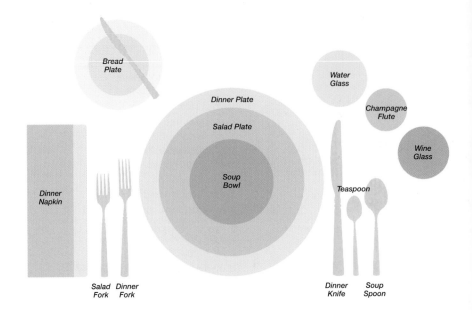

Bread Plate

Water Glass

Dinner Plate

Champagne Flute

Salad Plate

Wine Glass

Soup Bowl

Dinner Napkin

Teaspoon

Salad Fork

Dinner Fork

Dinner Knife

Soup Spoon

SOURCES

Bakers Twine
hobbylobby.com

Beads
joann.com
hobbylobby.com

Cardstock/Scrapbooking Supplies
memoryboundscrapbookstore.com
hobbylobby.com

Crafts Paint
deltacreative.com

Critter Boxes
Tuck Top Boxes
amazon.com

Felt
National Nonwovens
nationalnonwovens.com

Glue
Aleene's Tacky Glue
aleenes.com

Linoleum Block and Tools
amazon.com

Papers and Stickers
memoryboundscrapbookstore.com
michaels.com

Paper Tape/Ribbon
hobbylobby.com
michaels.com

Paper-Wrapped Floral Stems
michaels.com

Pearl Cotton
valdani.com

Ribbon
offray.com

Wire Wreath Form
Sumind 4 Wire
amazon.com

Wood Embroidery Hoops
hobbylobby.com

Wood Clothespins
amazon.com

Wood Cones
mylittlewoodshop
amazon.com

Wood Discs
amazon.com

Wood Dowel Tree
amazon.com

Wood Flat Bottom Balls
mylittlewoodshop
amazon.com

Wood Slices and Pieces
michaels.com
woodcrafter.com

Wool Pom-Poms
craftywoolfelt.com

Wrapping Papers
Society6.com
michaels.com

Wreath Moss
michaels.com

Yarn
yarnspirations.com
hobbylobby.com

CRAFT DESIGNERS

Judy Bailey • Melissa Belanger • Noah Burnley • Carol Field Dahlstrom • Roger Dahlstrom • Becky Grunwald • Kim Hutchison • Carey Johnson • Pam Koelling • Kylie Kurth (poem) • Matthew Mead • Krissa Rossbund • Suzonne Stirling • Jan Temeyer • Josh and Jenny Zacharewicz

INSIDE VERSE FOR CARD, PAGE 56

The sight of snowcapped evergreens,
and the scent of vanilla pine,
Bring rosy cheeks and tingling toes, and
footsteps crunching through the snow.

Wishing you a warm, cozy, and happy
holiday season.

by Kylie Kurth